generation eats

by
amyrosen

generation eats

GREAT RECIPES FOR A >>FAST FORWARD>>

CULTURE

WarwickPublishing
Toronto Los Angeles

ISBN 1-895629-91-8

Published by Warwick Publishing Inc.
388 King Street, West, Suite 111, Toronto, Ontario M5V 1K2
1424 North Highland Avenue, Los Angeles, CA 90027

Page design: Kimberley Young, mercer digital design
Photography: Bill Milne
Author photo: Joanna Sugar
Editorial Services: Harry Endrulat
Dishes & accessories courtesy of Pier 1 imports

Distributed by Firefly Books Ltd.
3680 Victoria Park Avenue, Willowdale, Ontario M2H 3K1

To mom, for being the perfect role model,
and dad, for his boyish enthusiasm.

contents

soups

salads

mains

contents

pizzas and pastas

desserts

breakfast

cocktails

foodstuff

introduct

We eat out, order in and take it on the run.

We travel light and have a taste for the exotic.

We're busy, lazy, stressed out and laid back.

We were latchkey kids and never learned how to cook.

We are health conscious but love dessert.

We are a generation of walking oxymorons.

We have short attention spans.

We have short attention sp—

We have discriminating palates but we eat fast food...

AND WE ARE HUNGRY.

ion

I have this theory: hunger is as much about our minds as our appetites, and eating means food for the brain *and* the body. Which is why the stove is as important to fine dining as the video machine.

Pop quiz: Are you as desperate for a gourmet pizza as you are for a luscious foreign film? Does your heart ache for a chocolatey confection coupled with a sizzling romance?

If the answer is yes (or maybe, – what the hell, I'll even take a no), you've come to the right book. Welcome to the world of *Generation Eats,* a place where food, film, and funny collide.

Here's my pitch: this is a cookbook like no other. Fresh and hip, it's half art, half food, and all attitude. Packed with over 80 original recipes ranging from breakfast to dessert, it also includes more than 250 video picks, a snazzy cocktail and wine section, is peppered with hints and tips, and brimming with inventive artwork by artist Malcolm Brown. It's also kind of funny, and maybe even a little smutty.

I wrote this book for people like me – people who like to cook, but hate doing dishes. People who eat healthy most of the time, but also know when it's time to indulge. Most of all, I wrote this book for people who don't know how to cook (including most of my friends), because it kills me to see them ordering in lousy food when they can be cooking themselves a great dinner in half the time it takes the delivery guy to show up with the soggy pizza box.

Most of these recipes are designed to serve two to four guinea pigs in under an hour, and trust me when I say you don't have to be a chef in order to whip up a great meal. In fact, I'm hoping I'm the one teaching you how to hard-boil an egg for the first time. And I want you to remember me as the one who taught you how to make good spaghetti sauce and fluffy cake from scratch.

But wait – there's more! For no money down, and no extra charge, I have selected the perfect movie picks for theme dining, romantic encounters, or just kicking back for a mellow evening. And my choices aren't just the usual blockbuster fare. I have included everything from heart-pounding film noir thrillers and sci-fi finds, to knee-slapping comedies and family fun; each highly rated so that you will never again be stuck with a dud. No more wasting valuable hours wandering aimlessly through video store ailes.

The choice is yours. You can either make a quick Salade Nicoise for yourself after a long day at work, or plan an Asian-themed feast for your pals, and shove *The Wedding Banquet* in the VCR while you all chow down. Each recipe is teamed up with three stellar video choices with informative blurbs detailing the finer points of the films.

So enjoy a read through, have a few laughs, learn some helpful tricks, and above all have fun while you're doing it. Because when you're zoned out in front of the tube watching *The World of Apu* as you eat the Tandoori Chicken and Dal that you've just prepared, you'll be glad you did. And so will your friends.

courtesy of Carmen Dunjko

appetizers, snacks, and sides

let's have a
BRUSCHETTA
Serves 6

Ingredients:

2 large tomatoes, chopped and drained
¼ cup fresh basil, chopped
2 cloves garlic, minced
pinch of salt
6 slices crusty Italian bread
1 tbsp. olive oil
fresh black pepper
shaved Parmesan cheese

Bruschetta is to the '90s what nachos were to the '80s. Except, the '80s sucke

toast!

Method:

1) To make tomato mixture, mix together tomatoes, chopped basil, garlic, and salt. Set aside.

2) Fire up the BBQ (or the broiler in the oven), then brush the top of each slice of bread with olive oil. Grill until toasted on one side, then do likewise on the flip side. Spoon tomato mixture over oiled side of bread, then crack fresh pepper and shave Parmesan cheese over top.

To Serve:

Arrange bruschetta on a nice big plate and have it sitting pretty on the coffee table when your guests arrive. This will stave off any hunger pangs until dinner's ready.

d, and the '90s are looking pretty delicious.

MOONSTRUCK: When the moon hits their eyes like a big pizza pie, a family of Italian-Americans go love crazy. Widow Cher is pursued by her fiancé's younger brother, until she can no longer resist the tortured soul (Nicolas Cage). Meanwhile, the rest of the family is having their own set of problems. A strikingly original comedy that won several Oscars, including a best actress nod for Cher. Dir: Norman Jewison. C: Cher, Nicolas Cage, Vincent Gardenia, Olympia Dukakis, Danny Aiello. 1987; 102 m.

THE GODFATHER II: A sequel that rivals the original? Truly a first. Past and present intertwine to gloriously carry on the saga of Don Corleone and his Mafia family. In this installment, the Don's son Michael (Al Pacino) takes over the family business, turning it into a well-tuned modern operation. Winner of seven Oscars. Dir: Francis Ford Coppola. C: Al Pacino, Robert Duvall, Diane Keaton, Robert De Niro, John Cazale, Talia Shire. 1974; 200 m.

ROMAN HOLIDAY: Talk about your nice-looking couples! In this fantastical romance, Audrey Hepburn plays a runaway princess who disguises herself as one of the common people to escape her royal duties in Rome. But eagle-eyed reporter Gregory Peck spots her and ends up falling for her. For this, her stunning debut, Hepburn won an Oscar. Dir: William Wyler. C: Audrey Hepburn, Gregory Peck, Eddie Albert, Tullio Carminati. 1953; 118 m.

HUMMUS WITH HOMEMADE PITA CRISPS
Serves 4

Ingredients:

2 small cloves of garlic, peeled and crushed
½ tsp. salt
19 oz. can of chickpeas, drained and rinsed
(reserve a handful for the garnish)
1 tbsp. tahini*
½ cup olive oil (reserve 1 tsp. for garnish)
¼ cup cold water
a few dashes Tabasco sauce
2 tbsp. lemon juice
¼ tsp. paprika (reserve ⅛ tsp. for pita crisps)
¼ tsp. cumin
4 pieces of fresh pita bread
1 tbsp. margarine
¼ tsp. garlic powder

*Tahini is an oily sesame paste. It is available at most specialty food shops and major supermarkets.

Sure they've had their troubles in the Middle East, but at least they have an alternative to potato chips. And it's healthy too – a miracle!

nk food:

Method:

1) Using a hand mixer or food processor, blend garlic with salt, add chickpeas, and mix until pureed. Mix in tahini.

2) Slowly drizzle the oil into the chickpea mixture and process until smooth. Next add the water until hummus reaches the desired porridgelike consistency. Add Tabasco, lemon juice, cumin, and paprika.

3) Transfer into a container, cover, and refrigerate.

4) Carefully rip pita breads in half, along the seams. Lay on counter, insides facing up, and smear some margarine on each piece. Shake a bit of salt, paprika, and garlic powder on top.

5) Cut each half into 4 wedges and place on cookie sheet.

6) Put in the oven under the broiler, leaving the door partially open. Keep an eye on them because it will take under a minute for the pita to turn crispy. Burn them, and they're toast.

To Serve:

Give each person 2 heaping tbsp. of hummus on a side plate. Drop a few chickpeas on top of the mound, drizzle with a bit of olive oil, and sprinkle with a shake of paprika. Arrange hot pita crisps in and around the hummus and dip in.

UNDER THE DOMIM TREE: Set on a kibbutz (where they eat a hell of a lot of hummus) in Israel during the '50s, it's a sentimental story about teenage orphans coming to terms with their Holocaust past and the future that awaits. A nice glimpse into Israeli culture, based on the autobiographical novel by Gila Almagor. Dir: Eli Cohen. C: Gila Almagor, Riki Blich, Ohad Knoller, Juliano Mer, Orli Perl, Eyal Sher. 1994; 102 m.

KADDISH: Five years in the making, this biting documentary chronicles the Nazis' "final solution" as seen through the eyes of a Holocaust survivor and his son. Bold, thoroughly engrossing — and you'll learn a thing or two. Dir: Steve Brand. 1989; 92 m.

PICNIC: A sexy drama based on William Inge's Pulitzer Prize-winning play. A charming drifter arrives on the scene and before long has the lady-folk doing cartwheels. An excellent depiction of life in small-town U.S.A. and what happens when someone new is added to the mix. Dir: Joshua Logan. C: William Holden, Rosalind Russel, Kim Novak, Betty Field. 1956; 113 m.

hot shots:
STUFFED JALAPENO PEPPERS
Makes 12 pieces

Ingredients:

6 jalapeno peppers
½ cup breadcrumbs
½ tsp. salt
¼ tsp. pepper
1 lb. block of cream cheese
1 cup vegetable oil
1 egg, beaten
salsa

Nuclear-hot chili peppers may set a 3-alarm blaze in your mouth, but the sm edge every time.

Method:

1) Put on some rubber gloves, then cut the ends off of the peppers and slice each one in half, lengthwise. Peel the seeds out, then pat each pepper dry with paper towel.

2) In a shallow plate, mix breadcrumbs with salt and pepper.

3) Take cream cheese out of the fridge, cut into 12 even pieces, then press a chunk into each half pepper.

4) Pour oil into a high-sided frying pan on medium-high heat. Meanwhile, dip each cheese-filled pepper in beaten egg, then roll in breadcrumbs.

5) Deep fry, turning often until golden brown. This shouldn't take more than a minute.

6) Drain on paper towel.

To Serve:

Line a plate with lettuce leaves and place the chili peppers on top, accompanied with salsa for dipping. And be sure to serve these tasty critters piping hot – I want to hear complaints of burnt mouths!

ooth cream cheese center pulls you back from the

THE ASSAULT: Winner of an Oscar for best foreign film, this Dutch heart-wrencher follows a man as he looks back on his childhood. Only his was no ordinary upbringing, as he was the only member of his family to escape the Nazis. Dir: Fons Rademakers. C: Derek DeLint, Marc Van Uchelen, Monique Van DeVan. 1986; 126 m.

BOTTLE ROCKET: I was howling with laughter when I caught this low-budget beauty in the theaters. Three Texan pals decide to take on a life of crime but are outrageously inept. Hilarity ensues. Like the film, these peppers have kick. Dir: Wes Anderson. C: Luke Wilson, Owen Wilson, Robert Musgrave, James Caan. 1996; 91 m.

THE EMPIRE STRIKES BACK: The best in the superlative sci-fi trilogy, all of the complicated exposition and story lines of Star Wars bear some fruit, and cutie-pie sage Yoda makes his big-screen debut. Talking action figures to follow. Dir: Irvin Kershner. C: Mark Hamill, Harrison Ford, Carrie Fisher, Billy Dee Williams. 1980; 124 m.

MUSHROOM
PATE

Makes 2 cups

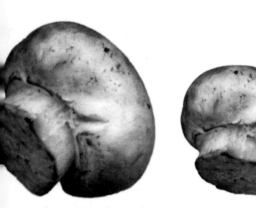

Ingredients:

(Preheat oven to 350 degrees Fahrenheit)

1 cup slivered almonds
1 small onion
1 garlic clove
¾ lb. fresh mushrooms
¼ cup butter
¾ tsp. salt
½ tsp. fresh cracked black pepper
¼ tsp. dried rosemary
1 tbsp. cognac (optional)
2 tbsp. olive oil

**Through the looking glass of your busy life, rich luxuries await. Go there, pic
pate over mini toasts. Then feel sorry for all of the little people.**

k[ ]and:

Method:

1) Spread almonds out on a cookie sheet and bake in the pre-heated 350 degree Fahrenheit oven until they turn light brown (about 7 minutes). Pour off pan into a bowl and let cool.

2) Using a food processor or hand blender, chop up the onions and garlic, then add mushrooms.

3) In a frying pan on medium heat, melt the butter and add the mushroom mixture. Stir and add salt, pepper, rosemary, and cognac. Turn up the heat to medium-high and cook until liquid has evaporated (this will take a while).

4) Process the almonds into fine crumbs, then gradually add the oil until a smooth paste forms. Add to the cooked mushroom mixture and stir until combined.

5) Pour into a lovely serving bowl, cover, and chill.

To Serve:

Put the bowl of pate in the center of a large plate filled with mini toasts (a type of cracker often called Paris Toasts). Make this one of several hors d'oeuvres you offer fellow revelers.

k up a snifter of cognac, and spread homemade

THE PARTY: Peter Sellers stars as an East Indian actor who mistakenly crashes a lavish Hollywood party and wreaks havoc in this slapstick-a-go-go. Throw your own party and be glad that klutzy Sellers isn't putting his paws in your pate. Dir: Blake Edwards. C: Peter Sellers. 1968; 99 m.

DON'S PARTY: Imagine, an intellectual Australian comedy! The scene is set as a group of middle classers (who are well versed in the one-upmanship of witty banter) gather to watch the election night results. Pate goes perfect with this film, as it is the number one food choice of snobs. Dir: Bruce Beresford. C: John Hargreaves, Pat Bishop, Graham Kennedy. 1976; 91 m.

THE INVITATION: An afternoon his coworkers will not soon forget, an office worker throws a garden party on the estate he is left by his dead mom. In dramatic twists and turns, his colleagues shed their skins, and we all become wiser because of it. Dainty finger sandwiches, mushroom pate, fresh lemonade, and a blanket and picnic hamper will set the mood nicely. Then all you have to do is haul the TV and VCR out onto the lawn. Dir: Claude Goretta. C: Jean-Luc Bideau, Francois Simon, Jean Champion. 1975; 100 m.

MEXICAN LAYERED DIP

Enough for a small party

Ingredients:

2 ripe avocados
2 green onions, chopped
1 lime, juiced
pinch of salt
½ cup mayonnaise
½ cup sour cream
½ a packet Mexican taco seasoning
1 can refried beans
1 cup Monterey Jack cheese, shredded
1 cup cheddar cheese, shredded
2 tomatoes, cored and diced
tortilla chips

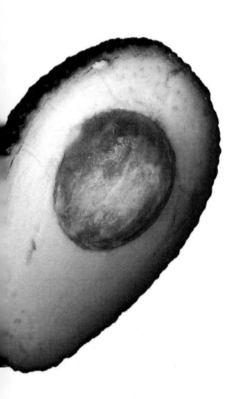

Make sure you have plenty of tortilla chips standing by, because it'll be a sh the excess dip with cupped hands. And they will do it, those locos.

on vegans:

Method:

1) Cut the avocados lengthwise, pull out the pit, and scoop out the avocado. Mash until smooth, add chopped green onions, lime juice, and salt. Mix together in bowl.

2) In another bowl, mix together the mayo, sour cream, and taco seasoning.

3) In a large decorative bowl, spread the can of refried beans on the bottom, top with the avocado mixture, then a layer of the Monterey Jack cheese, the mayonnaise mixture, the cheddar cheese, and finally, the diced tomatoes.

To Serve:

Set it out with a bowl of tortilla chips and let 'em go at it.

ame if your amigos have to resort to scooping up

EL NORTE: This drama traces the journey of a Guatemalan brother and sister team to El Norte – the U.S.A. Once in L.A., they learn some sad truths about their promised land. There are many layers that bring to bear the stunning look and compassion of the film. Same can be said for this delectable dip. Dir: Gregory Nava. C: Zaide Silvia Gutierrez, David Villalpando. 1983; 139 m.

LOS OLVIDADOS: Hailed as Luis Bunuel's most perfect film, it's a kinetic mixture of eroticism, action, drama, and crime. This is a serious piece of cinematic art. That director Bunuel, he's no dip. Dir: Luis Bunuel. C: Alfonso Mejia, Roberto Cobo, Stella Inda. 1950; 88 m.

TORTILLA FLAT: Based on John Steinbeck's robust novel, it's the tale of a group of men living in a California fishing village, whose chief aim in life is to avoid anything resembling work. Even they could muster up enough energy to pull off this dip. Dir: Victor Fleming. C: Spencer Tracy, Hedy Lamarr, John Garfield, Frank Morgan. 1942; 100 m.

GREEN TOMATOES AND GRAVY
Serves 4

Ingredients:

4 large green tomatoes (If you don't see any out on display, ask the produce manager to fetch some from the back. They are plentiful in the summer.)
½ cup flour
salt and pepper to taste
3 tbsp. butter
1 tbsp. vegetable oil
¼ cup brown sugar
½ small onion, minced
½ cup heavy cream (35%)

First comes the bite of sugary-crisp coating, then your teeth sink into the fles down your chin. This is what they call Southern hospitality. Better than the fi

ried, ma:

Method:

1) Wash, dry, and core tomatoes, then slice into ¼-inch slices.

2) On a large plate, mix flour with salt and pepper. Dip each side of each tomato slice in flour, then set on wire racks to dry for about 10 minutes.

3) Heat butter and oil in a large frying pan on medium-high heat, and when hot, add tomato slices. Brown on one side, flip over, and sprinkle with brown sugar. When crusty-cooked on bottom side, remove slices from pan and set aside on paper towel.

4) In the same pan fry minced onion for a few minutes, or until soft. Pour in cream, let boil until it reduces to a thickish sauce, then season with salt and pepper. Stir the sauce around, mixing in the scrapings from the sides and bottom of the pan.

To Serve:

Arrange tomato slices on a large plate, sugar side up, then pour the lip-smacking cream on top. Serve piping hot with an ice-cold brew.

hy tomato meat, and finally the creamy gravy drips m, at least better tasting.

FRIED GREEN TOMATOES: This wonderful drama, adapted from the Fannie Flagg novel, was one of the first successful chick flicks. By expertly using flashbacks, an elderly woman in a nursing home relays the Depression-era adventures of two young women to a Southern housewife. Much of the movie centers around the Whistle Stop Cafe, where they make juicy fried tomatoes, along with other specialties, including some one-of-a-kind barbecue! Dir: Jon Avnet. C: Kathy Bates, Mary Stuart Masterson, Mary-Louise Parker, Jessica Tandy. 1991; 120 m.

DELIVERANCE: Banjos were being plucked off of store shelves after the debut of this groundbreaking drama. From the James Dickey novel, a group of friends start out on a backwater canoe trip that turns into a nightmare full of banjo-strummin' inbreds. Ah, you've gotta love the South. Or at least the local grub. Dir: John Boorman. C: Jon Voight, Burt Reynolds, Ned Beatty, Ronny Cox. 1972; 109 m.

DRIVING MISS DAISY: An Oscar winner for best picture and actress (Jessica Tandy), it's the story of an elderly, argumentative Southern lady, and the 25-year friendship she forges with her quiet but devoted black chauffeur (Morgan Freeman). The unspoken love was nice, but her cook's tasty vittles were real scene stealers. Dir: Bruce Beresford. C: Morgan Freeman, Jessica Tandy, Dan Aykroyd. 1989; 99 m.

japanese min

COOL TOFU
APPETIZER
Serves 4

To prevent oil from splattering when you're frying, make sure the food is dry going in and the pan has high edges. If (GOD FORBID) you ARE hit with flying oil, put ice on the burn immediately.

Ingredients:

16 oz. package firm tofu
½ cup vegetable oil
1 tbsp. cornstarch
2 cups red cabbage, finely shredded
1 tbsp. fresh ginger, peeled and grated
1 small carrot, peeled and grated
2 green onions, finely chopped
1 tsp. sesame seeds (toasted optional)
2 tbsp. tamari sauce*

*Tamari is a richer, tastier version of soy sauce. It's aged and wheatless and can be found in major supermarkets.

It's sleek and stylish and made in Japan. No, it's not a Sony, it's an innovati it to the nearest karaoke bar. After dinner that is.

imalism:

Method:

1) Cut tofu into 8 even chunks (don't separate them yet) and drain on tea towel for 20 minutes.

2) Heat oil on high in a large frying pan. While the oil is getting hot, dip each tofu piece in cornstarch, making sure all sides are coated. Cook in hot oil until tofu becomes a pale brown, beige color. Drain on paper towel.

3) Prepare your cabbage, ginger, carrot, and green onion, but keep them each separate. If you're going to toast the seeds, now's the time.

4) On small side plates (Japanese-themed if you happen to have some) arrange shredded cabbage into little nests. Give each plate two pieces of cooked (but now cooled) tofu, top with some of the carrot, ginger, a sprinkling of green onion, and a couple tsp. of tamari. Top with a pinch of sesame seeds.

To Serve:

This goes great with miso soup (available at Asian markets and health food stores), some sushi, a big noodle dish, and loads of sake or Japanese beer. And it's a good idea to put a bottle of hot sauce or chili flakes on the table, so guests can get as hot as they want.

e starter that'll have your guests hightailing

THE BURMESE HARP: A Japanese antiwar film about a WWII veteran who goes on a soul-searching mission. He comes to terms with his past by burying war dead and turning to Buddhism. Watch the film, eat some tofu, and then go meditate. Dir: Kon Ichikawa. C: Shoji Yasui, Rentaro Mikuni. 1956; 116 m.

HARAKIRI: This action film soars above the ranks of trashy Hollywood blowup fare. A Japanese swordsman, who is about to commit ritual suicide, takes us on a sweeping journey through the feudal system and the events that brought him to this moment. A bit gory at times, so maybe finish eating before you turn it on. Dir: Masaki Kobayashi. C: Tatsuya Nakadai, Rentaro Mikuni, Tetsuro Tamba, Shima Iwashita. 1962; 135 m.

TAMPOPO: A Japanese knee-slapper that takes a cue from spaghetti-Westerns, with food-themed sketches thrown in for good taste. At the center of the film is a woman who discovers the secret to making perfect noodles, thanks to advice from a kindly truck driver. Dir: Juzo Itami. C: Ken Watanabe, Tsutomu Yamakazi, Nobuko Miyamoto. 1987; 95 m.

Let's Have a Toast! Bruschetta, page 14

keep you eyes on

SWEET POTATO "FRIES"
Serves 2

Ingredients:

(Preheat oven to 400 degrees Fahrenheit)

2 large sweet potatoes or yams
1 tbsp. olive oil
1 tsp. dried oregano
pinch of salt and pepper

Got a hankering for deep-fried taste, but trying to slim down to your Jenny what's missing.

30

these guys:

Method:

1) Scrub potatoes until clean, slice lengthwise into medium-sized wedges, then cut wedges in half. Place wedges in a small bowl, then toss well with the oil, oregano, and salt and pepper.

2) Bake the "fries" in the preheated 400 degree Fahrenheit oven for about 35 minutes, flipping halfway through baking.

To Serve:

Eat them as you would French fries – piping hot, with loads of ketchup or vinegar.

Craig size? Eat these: Only your scale will know

ANIMAL HOUSE: If you like vulgar, sophomoric humor, this is your flick. The boys of Delta fraternity at Faber College like their women, but not nearly as much as they like their beer. John Belushi is immortalized as party animal Bluto: "Food fight!" Dir: John Landis. C: John Belushi, Tim Matheson, John Vernon. 1978; 109 m.

REALITY BITES: I'll tell you, that Ethan does something to me. And for the fellows, there's the ever-appealing Winona. A group of twentysomethings, trying to find their way in the world, romp through this romantic comedy by way of a wicked soundtrack and sharp social commentary. Fries and ketchup go perfectly with Gen-X angst, don't you think? Dir: Ben Stiller. C: Winona Ryder, Ben Stiller, Ethan Hawke, Janeane Garofalo. 1994; 98 m.

FAST TIMES AT RIDGEMONT HIGH: This year in the life of a group of Southern California high schoolers is everything that TV's 90210 is not. Whether it's Spicoli (Sean Penn) getting pizza delivered to history class, or Judge Reinhold's turn as the upwardly mobile fast-food manager, there are as many laughs here as there are teens in malls. Dir: Amy Heckerling. C: Sean Penn, Jennifer Jason Leigh, Judge Reinhold. 1982; 91 m.

kick the can:

MEXICAN CORN BREAD

Makes 1 can-sized loaf

Ingredients:

(Preheat oven to 375 degree Fahrenheit)

1 egg, beaten
1 tbsp. sugar
⅓ cup milk
½ cup flour
½ cup cornmeal
1 ½ tsp. baking powder
¼ tsp. salt
1 jalapeno pepper, seeded and minced
½ cup of corn from a 14 oz. can of corn kernels, drained
(reserve can and peel off paper label)
vegetable oil spray

The cool thing about this bread is that you bake it up in a corn can to make

Method:

1) In a medium-sized bowl, combine egg, sugar, and milk

2) In another bowl, mix together flour, cornmeal, baking powder, and salt. Then add the dry ingredients to the bowl of wet ingredients. Mix well, then stir in the jalapeno pepper and corn kernels.

3) Take the corn can, peel off the label, then thoroughly dry the can. Give the inside a good spraying of vegetable oil spray, until completely coated, then pour in enough batter to fill the can almost to the top.

4) Put can in the preheated 375 degree Fahrenheit oven. The bread will rise up a bit, so make sure nothing is going to get in the way. Bake for 40 to 45 minutes, or until the top is golden brown and an inserted cake tester or knife comes out clean. Run a knife around the rim to loosen bread, then slide it out.

To Serve:

Slice the corn bread into 1-inch rounds and spread with butter. Goes great with breakfast, lunch, or dinner, and also makes a novel accompaniment to dips (For Gringos and Non-Vegans: Mexican Layered Dip recipe p.22).

kitschy little loafs. Reduce, reuse, recycle. Eat.

THE CORN IS GREEN: A hardcore drama about work versus education. Bette Davis eyes a young Welsh miner whom she grooms to win a university scholarship and a ticket out of their rough-edged Welsh village. Dir: Irving Rapper. C: Bette Davis, John Dall, Joan Lorring, Nigel Bruce. 1945; 114 m.

HIGH NOON: A classic Western about a newlywed lawman whose town abandons him as his rivals are due to arrive for a dual at high noon. The suspense is outrageous as the clock ticks and ticks closer to the hour of doom. Cooper was an Oscar-winner for his role. Dir: Fred Zinnemann. C: Gary Cooper, Grace Kelly, Lloyd Bridges. 1952; 84 m.

UNFORGIVEN: Clint Eastwood's masterful antithesis to the Western attacks the high esteem given to outlaw butchery and violence as a former killer comes back to town to take out the corrupt sheriff in Big Whisky. Way to go, Dirty Harry! The film swept the Oscars. Dir: Clint Eastwood. C: Clint Eastwood, Gene Hackman, Morgan Freeman, Richard Harris, Jaimz Woolvett, Frances Fisher. 1992; 130 m.

oy vay!
JEWISH VEGETABLE LATKES
Serves 6

KEEP WARM IN A PREHEATED 200° FAHRENHEIT OVEN IF NOT SERVING RIGHT AWAY.

Ingredients:

2 medium zucchini, grated
1 ½ tsp. salt (1 tsp. for draining zucchini and ½ tsp. for seasoning)
2 small sweet potatoes or yams, peeled and grated
1 small onion, grated
2 cloves garlic, minced
1 egg, beaten
½ cup flour
¼ tsp. black pepper
½ cup vegetable oil
apple sauce, sour cream, or yogurt for topping

In December, Jewish people celebrate Hanukkah while Christians celebrate t served in celebration of Hanukkah is fried potato pancakes (AKA latkes). Int

Method:

1) Place grated zucchini in a small colander in the sink. Stir in a tsp. of salt and let drain while you carry on with the rest of this recipe.

2) In a medium-sized bowl, mix together the grated sweet potatoes, onion, garlic, and egg. Then mix in flour, ½ tsp. salt, and pepper. Set aside.

3) After at least 15 minutes of draining time, scoop up handfuls of the zucchini and squeeze the liquid out of it, into the sink. Get it as dry as you can, then stir in with the prepared mixture.

4) Place a large frying pan over medium-high heat and add 2 tbsp. of the oil. When hot, drop in batter (a couple tbsp. for each latke) as if you're making small pancakes. Cook for several minutes on each side, until golden brown. Add more oil as needed. Place cooked latkes on paper towel to absorb excess oil.

To Serve:

Serve them hot along with a bowl of apple sauce and/or sour cream or yogurt for topping. Eat! You're all skin and bones! Take more, there's plenty. Maybe you don't like my cooking?

**hat lesser-publicized holiday. One of the dishes
erested in converting?**

EXODUS: From Leon Uris' sweeping novel about the creation of the state of Israel. A lavish production with terrific sets, exciting performances, and an Oscar-winning score. It's a longy but a goody. Dir: Otto Preminger. C: Paul Newman, Eva Marie Saint, Ralph Richardson, Peter Lawford, Lee Cobb, Sal Mineo. 1960; 213 m.

FIDDLER ON THE ROOF: Talk about your catchy musicals! From the Broadway smash about a Jewish dairyman in czarist Russia trying to cling to tradition. Serve the delectable latkes at sunrise or sunset. Dir: Norman Jewison. C: Topol, Norma Crane, Leonard Frey, Molly Picon, Paul Mann, Rosalind Harris, Michele Marsh. 1971; 181 m.

YENTL: A tour de force by Barbra Streisand, who wrote, produced, directed, and starred in this musical story. It's the tale of a woman who disguised herself as a man, in turn-of-the-century eastern Europe, so that she would be allowed to study the Torah. A lavish production and a treat to behold if you're a big Babs fan. Dir: Barbra Streisand. C: Barbra Streisand, Mandy Patinkin, Amy Irving. 1983; 134 m.

cheese balls

THE NO-BAKE STILTON DELIGHT

Makes about 15 pieces

Ingredients:

½ lb. Stilton cheese, left at room temperature until soft
2 tbsp. butter, softened
2 tbsp. fresh parsley, chopped
⅛ tsp. cayenne pepper
½ cup walnuts, crushed into crumbs
1 large plate of prepared fresh fruit (apples, grapes, strawberries, etc.)

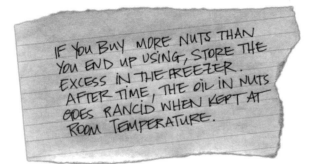

IF YOU BUY MORE NUTS THAN YOU END UP USING, STORE THE EXCESS IN THE FREEZER. AFTER TIME, THE OIL IN NUTS GOES RANCID WHEN KEPT AT ROOM TEMPERATURE.

These are terrific little lovelies to eat with libations at a cocktail party, and man on the moon and who knows who else.

Method:

1) Mix together the Stilton cheese and butter until smooth. Stir in parsley and cayenne, then check for seasoning.

2) Spread walnut crumbs out on a plate and form cheese mixture into 1-inch balls. Roll cheese mixture in crumbs, then chill in the fridge for at least an hour before serving.

To Serve:

Place the balls on a tray, surrounded by prepared fresh fruit. And wouldn't those little frilly toothpicks be a kick?

best of all, no fuss, no muss. A little treat from the

NIGHT SHIFT: A hilarious comedy that pits freethinking Michael Keaton (in a breakout performance) against Henry Winkler's staid morgue attendant. The two partners get talked into a pimping deal by sugary hooker Shelley Long, whereupon they stage an impromptu party at the morgue, where I'm certain they served classy stilton balls. Dir: Ron Howard. C: Henry Winkler, Michael Keaton, Shelley Long. 1982; 105 m.

BLUE VELVET: Blue cheese, a blue moon, and blue velvet will make for a moody-themed evening for you and a partner. From the twisted mind of David Lynch, it's a scary crime thriller about a small-town boy who gets sucked into the warped world of a nightclub singer and her sadistic stalker. Dir: David Lynch. C: Kyle MacLachlan, Isabella Rossellini, Dennis Hopper, Laura Dern. 1986; 120 m.

WITHNAIL AND I: This is one of my all-time favorites. Starving actors living in a condemned London flat take off to the country for a little R&R. But once in the wilderness (albeit sheltered by a gorgeous summer home) they realize they lack important survival skills, like where to get food without a chip shop? Dir: Bruce Robinson. C: Richard E. Grant, Paul McGann, Richard Griffiths. 1986; 108 m.

popeye goes

SPICED SPINACH, SAUTÉ
Serves 4

Ingredients:

2 large potatoes, peeled and chopped into 1-inch cubes
2 large carrots, peeled and chopped into ½-inch rounds
2 tbsp. butter
5 shallots, peeled and thinly sliced
3 garlic cloves, minced
2 tbsp. ginger, peeled and julienned*
1 tbsp. cumin
1 tbsp. curry
2 lbs. fresh spinach leaves, stems removed
salt and pepper to taste

* To "julienne" means to slice into tiny matchsticks.

So, maybe that sailor never went to India. What are you, a cop? Look, this is one little inaccuracy.

Indian:

Method:

1) Put potatoes and carrots in a medium-sized saucepan, add enough water to cover veggies, and cook on high heat, partially covered, for about 15 minutes. When cooked, set aside but don't drain until using.

2) In a large frying pan, melt butter over medium heat, add shallots and garlic, and cook for about 3 minutes, or until browned.

3) Stir in ginger, cumin, and curry, cook for 20 seconds, reduce heat to medium-low, then toss in spinach, little by little, stirring around until it's all wilted. Add cooked potatoes and carrots, salt and pepper, and mix well.

To Serve:

A great side dish to tandoori chicken, rice, and buttered nan bread. It's like there's a party going on in your mouth, and everyone's invited!

so tasty, so easy, so healthy, you'll allow me this

MISSISSIPPI MASALA: She's an Indian immigrant, he's a black businessman, and together they are outcasts. The touchy topic of racism is magnificently brought to life in this insightful yet sensuous look at racial prejudice in the South. The subject matter may be rough, but that Denzel Washington is easy on the eyes. Dir: Mira Nair. C: Denzel Washington, Roshan Seth, Sarita Choudhury, Charles S. Dutton, Tico Wells, Joe Seneca. 1991; 117 m.

THE WORLD OF APU: In this, the final installment in Satyajit Ray's monumental trilogy, our hero matures into fatherhood but then loses his footing once again. Stellar performances in an unforgettable film. It's a shame that the Academy waited until he was on his deathbed to finally acknowledge Ray's contribution to world cinema. Dir: Satyajit Ray. C: Soumitra Chatterjee, Sharmila Tagore. 1959; 103 m.

DINNER AT EIGHT: An all-time comedy classic, adapted from the Broadway hit for this regal cast. Secrets and lies, forks and knives. Put together a full-on fancy five-course dinner party, complete with candlelight, name cards, and napkin rings, when you dish out this charmer. Dir: George Cukor. C: John Barrymore, Wallace Beery, Marie Dressler, Jean Harlow. 1933; 111 m.

Cheese Balls: The No-Bake Stilton Delight, page 36

potato proza

MASHED TATERS
Serves 4

Ingredients:

4 large all-purpose potatoes, each peeled and
cut into 8 chunks
1 tbsp. unsalted butter
¾ cup sharp cheddar cheese, grated
10 small pimento-filled green olives, sliced
1 tbsp. olive oil
¼ cup warm milk
1 tsp. dried oregano
salt and pepper to taste

DIFFERENT VARIETIES OF MASHED
POTATOES ARE USED FOR VARIOUS
PURPOSES. YUKON GOLD ARE
OPTIMAL FOR MAKING BOILED OR
MASHED POTATOES, RED ONES
ARE GREAT FOR BROILING AND
BARBECUING, BAKING POTATOES
ARE TERRIFIC FOR — YOU GUESSED
IT — BAKING, AND RUSSET POTATOES
ARE FINE EVERY WHICH WAY.

You lust after French fries, but your ab machine is rusting away in the closet. Mashed potatoes satisfy every emotional need in about 10 minutes.

Method:

1) Place peeled, chunked potatoes in a medium-sized pot full of cold water. Make sure the water covers the potatoes. Bring to a boil, lower the heat to medium-low, and simmer the potatoes for 15 to 20 minutes or until a fork glides through them.

2) Drain the potatoes in a colander, then put them back in the pot and mash with a big fork or a potato masher if you have one.

3) Stir in butter until it melts, then add the cheese, olives, oil, milk, oregano, and salt and pepper. Heat on low for 2 minutes.

To Serve:

Serve a heaping load alongside your favorite main dish or have a bowlful for a comforting lunch.

You feel alienated, and Mommy is far away.

CLOSE ENCOUNTERS OF THE THIRD KIND: Spielberg's pre-E.T. sci-fi flick paints a similar picture of aliens — they're the good guys, and we're the dopes. Richard Dreyfuss is perfect as a man who becomes obsessed with hitching a ride with the extraterrestrials. Check out the scene where he sculpts a likeness of the coming spaceship out of a plate of mashed potatoes. Dir: Steven Spielberg. C: Richard Dreyfuss, Francois Truffaut, Teri Garr, Melinda Dillon. 1977; 132 m.

MY OWN PRIVATE IDAHO: A very different road movie in which two male prostitutes — a narcoleptic male and a wealthy bisexual — forge a special friendship as they search for meaning in their troubled lives. It's one part black comedy, one part drama, and all heart. Dir: Gus Van Sant. C: Keanu Reeves, River Phoenix, William Richert. 1991; 110 m.

ONE POTATO, TWO POTATO: A real groundbreaker that takes on prejudices as Barbara Barrie and Bernie Hamilton fight to keep her kids, when the ex-husband sues for custody. So honest it'll leave a bitter taste in your mouth. Dir: Larry Peerce. C: Barbara Barrie, Bernie Hamilton, Richard Mulligan. 1964; 92 m.

GRILLED CHICKEN SATAY
Serves 2

Ingredients:

2 tbsp. + 1 tsp. soy sauce
1 tbsp. + 1 tsp. rice vinegar
2 boneless, skinless chicken breasts, each cut
into 4 even, long strips
2 tbsp. smooth peanut butter
3 tbsp. warm water
1 clove garlic, crushed
1 tsp. sesame oil
¼ tsp. chili flakes
8 wooden or metal skewers
1 green onion, chopped

NEVER PUT COOKED MEAT BACK ON THE SAME PLATE YOU USED BEFORE COOKING IT. ALWAYS USE A CLEAN PLATE AND UTENSILS TO AVOID ICKY CONTAMINATION.

This was the title of a major motion picture that never saw the light of day, seductively archaic about eating food off of a stick. Who knows, maybe the c satay sauce back then.

anuts:

Method:

1) In a medium-sized bowl, stir together 2 tbsp. soy sauce and a tbsp. of rice vinegar, then add chicken strips, stir, and let marinate for a minimum of 30 minutes.

2) Now to make the satay sauce. In a small bowl, combine peanut butter, water, a tsp. of rice vinegar, a tsp. soy sauce, the garlic, the sesame oil, and chili flakes. Mix it up until nice and smooth.

3) Skewer marinated chicken strips onto 8 skewers, through the length of the pieces. If you're using wooden ones (found in Oriental markets) they must be soaked for about an hour before using. Broil a few inches from the heat for 2 to 3 minutes on each side, or until juices run clear.

To Serve:

Layer grilled chicken skewers on a plate, sprinkle with green onion, and transfer satay sauce into an attractive little bowl. Chopped red pepper and cucumber marinated in rice wine vinegar with a pinch of sugar makes a nice side for the satay.

so I made it into a recipe. And there's something avemen would have chosen not to evolve if they had

PLATOON: Winner of a handful of Oscars, including best picture, it's one of the best films ever made about the war in Vietnam. Charlie Sheen stars as a well-meaning wealthy kid who joins the army to become a real person. He narrates the film as bombs tear up his friends and infighting all but destroys his platoon. A tour de force by director Oliver Stone, before his conspiracy-theory-loony days. Dir: Oliver Stone. C: Tom Berenger, Willem Dafoe, Charlie Sheen, Forest Whitaker. 1986; 120 m.

REBEL WITHOUT A CAUSE: You've got an urge to eat spicy meat on a stick, and you don't know why. It's just who you are. James Dean feels much the same in this '50s generational movie about alienated teens. All of the misunderstood leads died tragic real-life deaths. Eerie. Dir: Nicholas Ray. C: James Dean, Natalie Wood, Sal Mineo. 1955; 111 m.

PEE-WEE'S BIG ADVENTURE: So he got caught with his hands down his pants, give the guy a break! Making the successful leap from his playhouse to the big screen, Pee-Wee (Paul Reubens) goes on a wacky adventure to track down his prized bicycle. Innovative stuff a la director Tim Burton, this film is one the whole family can enjoy. Dir: Tim Burton. C: Pee-Wee Herman, Elizabeth Daily, Mark Holton, Diane Salinger. 1981; 90 m.

did you know it

TOMATOES PROVENCALE
Serves 2

Ingredients:

(Preheat oven to 400 degrees Fahrenheit)

2 garlic cloves, chopped
2 tbsp. breadcrumbs
1 tbsp. parsley, chopped
2 tsp. olive oil
pinch of salt and pepper
1 large tomato

**It's the attack of the killer tomatoes!
By "killer," I mean good.**

's a Fruit?

Method:

1) Place chopped garlic on a cutting board and pour bread-crumbs on top. Add parsley and chop everything together until very fine. Put in a little bowl, mix in the oil, and add salt and pepper to taste.

2) Cut tomato in half across the middle, then cut a thin slice off the bottom of each half, so that they stand upright. Place in a little Pyrex dish, sprinkle tomatoes with salt and pepper, then top with breadcrumb mixture.

3) Bake in the preheated 400 degree Fahrenheit oven for about 5 minutes, or until hot and soft, but not mushy.

To Serve:

This is the perfect accompaniment to a grilled steak or fish dish.

INDOCHINE: This French mover stars Catherine Deneuve as a woman in 1930s Indochina who is at odds with her adopted daughter and the political turmoil of the time. A lustily colorful film that you won't be throwing tomatoes at. It won an Oscar for the best of the foreign entries. Dir: Regis Wargnier. C: Catherine Deneuve, Vincent Perez, Linh Dan Pham, Jean Yanne, Dominique Blanc. 1992; 155 m.

THE MAN WHO CAME TO DINNER: An old-time comedy that has a snobbish critic and radio personality stranded in a small Midwestern town, after he takes a tumble. He is completely arrogant and makes life miserable for those who surround him. Check out the frumpy secretary; it's Bette Davis! Dir: William Keighley. C: Bette Davis, Ann Sheridan, Monty Woolley, Billie Burke, Jimmy Durante. 1941; 112 m.

PARIS IS BURNING: An enthralling documentary that takes us on a tour of the male transvestite subculture of New York City. They get all dolled up and romp through lavish balls in which they pose as everything from models to marines. Very funny, very sad, and totally lovely. Dir: Jennie Livingston. 1990; 78 m.

CALIFORNIA-STYLE QUESADILLAS
Enough for a mid-sized party

Ingredients:

(Preheat oven to 200 degrees Fahrenheit)

8 oz. cream cheese, softened
1 ripe mango, peeled and chopped
½ lime, juiced
½ tsp. sugar
2 large jalapeno peppers, seeded and minced
1 cup cooked baby shrimp (fresh is best, but canned is okay)
20 8-inch flour tortillas
2 cups shredded mozzarella cheese
3 tbsp. vegetable oil

Concoct these cheesy-sweet wedges for the best in fusion fare. Crisp on the o piping hot in the middle, these snacks are hotter than the apple filling in Mc

an bites:

Method:

1) Mix together cream cheese, mango, lime, sugar, and jalapeno peppers. Stir in shrimp.

2) Take a tortilla and spread a heaping tbsp. of the cream cheese mixture over the surface. Top with a sprinkling of shredded mozzarella, then cover with another tortilla.

3) In a medium-sized frying pan, heat a teaspoon of oil over medium heat. Place the quesadilla in the hot oil and cook until brown (about 1 minute). Flip and fry until browned on the other side. Push down with spatula, remove from pan, drain on paper towel, then put on cookie sheet.

4) Repeat step #3 for the remaining 9 quesadillas, adding more oil as needed. When all have been fried, put the cookie sheet(s) in the preheated 200 degree Fahrenheit oven to keep them hot until your guests arrive.

To Serve:

Cut each quesadilla into 4 wedges and pile 'em high on several plates for easy access. Serve with salsa and Corona beer with lime wedges to wash down the spicy kick.

tside and
Donalds' pies.

USE CAUTION WHEN WORKING WITH ANY TYPE OF SPICY PEPPER. DO THE DEED CAREFULLY AND QUICKLY, MAKING SURE NOT TO TOUCH YOUR EYES OR ANY OTHER ORIFICE DURING THE PROCESS. THEN WASH YOUR HANDS WELL, WITH SOAP AND WATER.

rice the red

PINEAPPLE FRIED RICE

Serves 6

Ingredients:

½ tbsp. + 1 ½ tbsp. vegetable oil
2 large eggs, beaten with 1 tbsp. water
3 green onions, chopped
1 red pepper, cored and chopped
14 oz. can pineapple chunks, drained
10 oz. can sliced mushrooms, drained
¼ cup canned, sliced water chestnuts
½ cup frozen sweet peas, thawed
1 cup bean sprouts
3 cups cooked rice (follow instructions on box)
4 tbsp. soy sauce
1 tsp. sugar
1 tsp. sesame oil

Make your own Chinese food and forget the 45-minute wait for the delivery "Hey, save me the leftovers."

antern:

Method:

1) Heat ½ tbsp. of oil on medium-high heat in a wok. Add the eggs and fry, without stirring, for about a minute. Flip and cook the other side. When eggs are fully cooked, remove from wok and chop into chunks.

2) Pour remaining oil into wok, heat on high, and add the onions, red pepper, pineapple, mushrooms, water chestnuts, peas, and bean sprouts. Stir-fry for several minutes, add rice, egg, soy sauce, sugar, and sesame oil, then stir-fry for 2 more minutes.

To Serve:

Pour rice into a serving bowl and serve hot with other Oriental delicacies, like Cantankerous Corn: Corn And Crab Soup (p.68) and Moody Crustaceans: Sweet And Sour Shrimp (p.142).

guy with the soggy takeout bags. Confucius says,

TEA AND RICE: The tradition of arranged marriages is put to the test as a miserable recipient of one pleads with her niece to go against her parents' wishes so that she has a chance at happiness. A sensational drama that explores some age-old Japanese traditions — much like green tea and rice. Dir: Yasujiro Ozu. C: Shin Saburi, Michiyo Kogure, Koji Tsurata. 1964; 115 m.

RAISE THE RED LANTERN: This Chinese beauty colorfully chronicles the life of a 1920s woman who agrees, at her mother's request, to marry a rich man and become mistress number four. Based on the book by Su Tong. Dir: Zhang Yimou. C: Gong Li, Ma Jingwu, He Caifei, Cao Cuifeng. 1991; 125 m.

THE FLAVOR OF GREEN TEA OVER RICE: A Japanese drama in which a childless, aging couple, who bicker constantly, realize their importance to each other when the husband goes out of town. Dir: Yasujiro Ozu. C: Shin Saburi, Michiyo Kogure. 1953; 115 m.

Snack of the Gods: Feta and Red Pepper Dip, page 60

seasoned 'ui

SUGAR-
SPICED
NUTS

Makes 3 cups

Ingredients:

4 tbsp. vegetable oil
3 cups whole almonds (not roasted)
½ cup brown sugar
2 tsp. cumin powder
2 tsp. chili flakes
2 tsp. sesame seeds
1 tsp. kosher salt*

*Kosher or coarse salt is chunky-style salt that can
be found in the spice section of supermarkets.

These Middle Eastern-style almonds go great with mint tea as a meal topper

natics:

Method:

1) In a large nonstick frying pan, heat oil on medium, add almonds, and stir with a wooden spoon until coated with oil. Sprinkle brown sugar over the nuts, and mix together until sugar melts and the almonds are coated and slightly browned. It will take 4 to 5 minutes. Then turn off heat, sprinkle nuts with cumin, chili flakes, sesame seeds, and salt, and toss about.

2) Pour sugar-coated nuts onto a cookie sheet, making sure they're all separated. Allow to cool for an hour before serving.

To Serve:

Just pour the tasty nuggets into nut bowls, but keep them away from compulsive eaters.

...or a cold brew anytime. Think global, eat local.

THE HARD NUT: These delicious nuts may be hard, but they're also sweet, salty, and spicy. As for the movie, it falls under the same description. The famous Mark Morris Dance Group presents a hilarious song and dance adaptation of Tchaikovsky's The Nutcracker. Like the almonds, it's a departure from the norm. C: Mark Morris Dance Group. 1991; 90 m.

RISKY BUSINESS: This sharp satire launched the career of Tom Cruise and sent Rayban and Fruit of the Loom stocks soaring. A teenager in need of some fast cash turns his house into a bordello, with help from hooker girlfriend Rebecca DeMornay, while his parents are away. Risky, but not as venturesome as these crazy nuts. Dir: Paul Brickman. C: Tom Cruise, Rebecca DeMornay, Curtis Armstrong, Bronson Pinchot. 1983; 99 m.

PSYCHO: Don't go into the shower alone, there are nuts out there! This quintessential Alfred Hitchcock shocker was a trailblazer for every psychological thriller that followed. It's some scary stuff, so keep a pillow standing by in case you have to cover your eyes. Dir: Alfred Hitchcock. C: Anthony Perkins, Janet Leigh, Vera Miles, John Gavin. 1960; 109 m.

GRILLED POLENTA WITH CREAMY GORGONZOLA TOMATO SAUCE

Serves 4

Ingredients:

1 tube (2.2 lbs.) prepared polenta (cut into 10 even rounds)*
vegetable oil spray
2 tbsp. tomato sauce (prepared or homemade)
3 ½ oz. Gorgonzola cheese (reserve ¼ of it)
⅓ cup table cream (18%)
¼ cup dry white wine
salt and pepper to taste

*Polenta is a northern Italian staple made from cooked corn-meal. It is available at most specialty supermarkets and looks like a really big, really thick roll of yellow cookie dough.

IF THE SAUCE TURNS OUT TO BE TOO RUNNY, MIX A TSP. OF CORNSTARCH WITH A TBSP. OF WINE OR CREAM, THEN STIR INTO SAUCE.

Okay, you want to impress that special someone, but you're still not ready to Call me in the morning.

Method:

1) Spray both sides of each polenta slice with vegetable oil and cook on a heated BBQ or in the oven on a cookie sheet on high heat (450 degrees Fahrenheit). Cook for approximately 5 minutes on each side, then remove from grill (or oven) and set aside. If you're using the oven, broil the top side of the polenta until it browns a bit.

2) In a small saucepan over medium-low heat, mix together the tomato sauce, cheese, cream, and wine. Cook the sauce until it's blended and hot, but not boiling. Taste it, then add as much salt and pepper as you think necessary.

To Serve:

Layer two slices of cooked polenta on each plate, then spoon a healthy serving of the sauce on top. Sprinkle with crumbled Gorgonzola and serve.

commit to slave-cooking for hours. Try this.

BEFORE SUNRISE: A supremely engaging love story that speaks to my generation. Two soul mates meet by chance on a Vienna-bound train. They spend only one night together, but what a night it is; talking, eating, and lovemaking galore. Everyone deserves to have an evening like this. If you happen to be short the plane fare to Europe, the $100 train ticket, and the unbelievable mate-meeting luck, the polenta should suffice. Dir: Richard Linklater. C: Ethan Hawke, Julie Delpy. 1995; 100 m.

FLIRTING: A low-budget Australian-made charmer in which a shy boy falls for a gorgeous, outspoken Ugandan exchange student. This sensitive comedy set in the '60s will definitely get that special someone in the mood, when coupled with this delicate yet sensual polenta. Dir: John Duigan. C: Noah Taylor, Thandie Newton, Nicole Kidman. 1990; 100 m.

TRUST: You either love Hal Hartley's stuff or you hate it. You get him or you don't. I do, and so should you. In this picture, an angry, abused man, and a wayward young woman meet and fall head over heels. The humor is as dry as the Sahara and as engaging as tomato Gorgonzola sauce. Dir: Hal Hartley. C: Adrienne Shelly, Martin Donovan, Merritt Nelson. 1991; 105 m.

smorgasbord
ANTIPASTO PLATTER
Serves 4 to 6

Ingredients:

1 lb. fresh mussels in the shell
1 large lemon, juiced, + 1 tsp. of its lemon zest
2 cloves of garlic, crushed
½ tsp. chili flakes
½ medium cauliflower
14 oz. can crushed tomatoes
a bunch of fresh basil leaves
1 tbsp. olive oil
1 small onion, finely chopped
14 small, pitted black olives, sliced
1 tsp. dried oregano
1 tsp. sugar
1 small green pepper, cored and diced
pinch of salt and pepper
2 medium tomatoes, cored and sliced
4 balls of bocconcini cheese (young mozzarella), sliced
a handful of assorted spiced olives (available at specialty stores and large supermarkets)
2 roasted red peppers (bottled in oil or water), sliced
1 small jar bottled artichoke hearts

Method:

1) First we'll get started on the mussels so that they'll have time to cool. Scrub mussels under cold water to remove any sand or grit. Place a medium pot of water on the stove and bring to a simmer (the water won't be boiling, but a little jumpy). Put mussels in water and remove them as their shells open. Throw out any mussels that don't pop open of their own free will. Rinse under cool water.

2) Using your hands, open the cooked mussels, separating the shell halves from each other. Then, using a small sharp knife or scissors, carefully loosen the mussels from their shells. Place each one on a half shell, discarding unused shells. Then, in a small bowl combine lemon juice, garlic, and chili flakes. Spoon a bit over each mussel, place on a cookie sheet, and grill until heated through. Watch them; this won't take long.

3) Carefully arrange mussels at one end of the platter you'll be using to serve the antipasto. Sprinkle with lemon zest, cover with plastic wrap, and put in the fridge.

4) Wash cauliflower and break into large florets. Put in a medium-sized pot, cover with water, and boil until fork-tender (about 15 minutes). Drain in a colander and rinse under cold water.

A little nosh before the main attraction (am I mixing my allusions here or wh smack your hand for snacking. Sven, that's amore!

italiano:

5) Using a hand blender, puree crushed tomatoes with 3 basil leaves. Then, in a medium frying pan, heat oil, add chopped onion, cook for 2 minutes, add sliced olives and green pepper, cook for 2 more minutes, and then pour in the tomato puree. Add 1 tsp. of sugar and a pinch of salt and pepper. Cook over medium heat for 3 minutes, then toss in drained cauliflower florets. Stir around until the cauliflower in completely coated. Remove from heat and set aside.

To Serve:

Now it's time to assemble the whole damn thing. Take the platter out of the fridge and arrange the tomato and bocconcini slices into a fan on the platter, alternating between tomato slice, bocconcini slice, and basil leaf. Then drizzle with a bit of olive oil. Find spots for the mound of sliced peppers, mixed olives, drained jar of artichoke hearts, and the red and white cauliflower. Just arrange the food so that it looks appetizing, adding your own nice touches, like some basil leaves for garnish. When your guests arrive, give them a glass of wine in one hand and a side plate in the other. They'll know what to do.

at?). A bite of this, taste of that, and Mama doesn't

THE GODFATHER: The lurid world of the Mafia is brought to life in this gripping film, adapted from Mario Puzo's best-selling novel. Top-notch entertainment and cinematic art set the stage nicely for an Italian feast. A multiple Oscar winner. Dir: Francis Ford Coppola. C: Marlon Brando, Al Pacino, James Caan, Diane Keaton. 1972; 175 m.

THE BICYCLE THIEF: An Italian landmark film in the neorealist tradition. A father and son spend a day in Rome, searching for their stolen bicycle. This is an incredibly moving drama about what we're capable of when faced with an extreme situation. Watch for the heartwarming scene in which little Bruno and his father treat themselves to a lavish lunch. Dir: Vittorio De Sica. C: Lamberto Maggiorani, Lianella Carell, Enzo Staiola. 1948; 89 m.

GOODFELLAS: Brutally violent, rib-tickling funny, and sensitive, all at the same time. Based on the book by Nicholas Pileggi, it covers 30 years in the life of a New York Mafia family. The fast pacing and excellent cast suck you right in. And the scene where the gang stops off for a bite at Joe Pesci's mom's house (actually Martin Scorsese's real life mama) is utterly delectable. Dir: Martin Scorsese. C: Robert De Niro, Joe Pesci, Ray Liotta, Lorraine Bracco, Paul Sorvino. 1990; 148 m.

snack of the

FETA AND RED PEPPER DIP

Serves 4

Ingredients:

6 oz. feta cheese, crumbled (a tsp. reserved for garnish)
¼ cup bottled roasted red peppers, drained and chopped
1 garlic clove, minced
1 tsp. lemon juice
2 tsp. olive oil
⅛ tsp. cayenne pepper
1 tbsp. parsley, chopped (for garnish)

Being the leader of the Olympian that he liked to nosh on this tasty mountaintop.

gods:

Method:

1) Combine first 6 ingredients and puree with a hand blender.

To Serve:

Pour into a ceramic dish and top with reserved feta and parsley.
Serve with pita crisps (recipe p.16) or warm, Greek-style pita
bread for ripping and dipping.

gods gave Zeus a king-sized hunger. Legend has it
wonder before launching lightning bolts from the

MEDITERRANEO: This succulent Italian comedy takes us on a tour of a Greek island, where a group of stranded WWII Italian soldiers come to love this piece of paradise. They eat, swim, fall in love, and don't want to leave their picturesque play-ground come the war's end. Won the Oscar for best foreign film. Dir: Gabriele Salvatores. C: Diego Abatantuono, Claudio Bigagli, Giuseppe Cederna, Claudio Bisio. 1991; 90 m.

SHIRLEY VALENTINE: So you're stuck in a rut, making bangers and mash for your idiot hus-band, and so bored that the walls have become your best friends. What do you do? Take off to Greece and reinvent yourself. like our heroine, who is immediately wooed by a sexy Greek restaurateur. A sun-baked awakening. Dir: Lewis Gilbert. C: Pauline Collins, Tom Conti, Julia McKenzie, Joanna Lumley. 1989; 160 m.

ZORBA THE GREEK: A swash-buckling man lives his life to the fullest in a small Greek vil-lage in Crete. His spirit washes off on the people around him, especially a visiting English writer. An Oscar winner three times over. Dir: Michael Cacoyannis. C: Anthony Quinn, Alan Bates, Irene Papas, Lila Kedrova, George Foundas. 1964; 142 m.

HOT ARTICHOKE DIP

Serves 6 to 8

Ingredients:

(Preheat oven to 350 degrees Fahrenheit)

1 package frozen spinach, thawed and chopped
6 oz. jar artichoke hearts, drained and chopped
1 cup grated mozzarella cheese
2 garlic cloves, minced
2 tsp. lemon juice
1 tbsp. mayonnaise
½ tsp. salt
¼ tsp. pepper
Melba toast

This superb mélange of artichokes, spinach, and mozzarella cheese makes a
ing of palates. But between you and me, do you really know anyone who br

eese:

Method:

1) Squeeze the excess water out of the spinach, then mix all of the ingredients together in an attractive ovenproof dish. Bake in the preheated 350 degree Fahrenheit oven for about 45 minutes or until golden brown on top.

To Serve:

Serve steaming hot, surrounded by Melba toast or sliced baguette for spreading. Warning: This stuff is highly addictive.

THIS DIP IS EVEN BETTER WHEN THE INGREDIENTS ARE MIXED TOGETHER AHEAD OF TIME. IT'S ALSO A REAL TIME SAVER. PREPARE A DAY IN ADVANCE, AND 45 MINUTES BEFORE THE GANG ARRIVES, POP IT IN THE OVEN.

party-pleasing nibble for even the most discriminat-
ngs a discriminating palate to a good party?

BABETTE'S FEAST: This haunting Danish Oscar winner is a feast for the eyes as well as the soul. Set in 18th-century Denmark, two elderly sisters, religious to the core, begrudgingly allow their expatriate French cook to prepare a lavish meal with her lottery winnings. The film looks good enough to eat, but you'll be full from the dip. Dir: Gabriel Axel. C: Stephane Audran, Jean-Philippe Lafont, Bibi Andersson, Birgitte Federspiel. 1987; 102 m.

THE CONVERSATION: What goes better with dinner than a little conversation? Especially if it's this enthralling drama about a professional wiretap-per whose investigation unearths a complicated murder plot. Nail-biting tension throughout. Dir: Francis Ford Coppola. C: Gene Hackman, Frederic Forrest, John Cazale. 1974; 113 m.

WHEN A STRANGER CALLS: This crime flick is the sole reason why I never made a cent off of babysitting. Still it haunts me: "Have you checked the chil-dren?" Maybe if babysitter Carol Kane had prepared some of this luscious dip to offer the intruder, those kids would still be alive. But probably not. Dir: Fred Walton. C: Carol Kane, Charles Durning, Colleen Dewhurst. 1979; 97 m.

courtesy of Kevin Denny

soups

body boost:

CARROT-ORANGE-GINGER SOUP
Serves 4

Ingredients:

3 tbsp. butter
2 large onions, chopped
2 garlic cloves, minced
1 tbsp. fresh ginger, peeled and minced (or 2 tsp. ginger powder)
2 cups chicken stock
8 large carrots, peeled and chopped
2 apples, peeled, cored, and chopped
2 cups orange juice
salt and pepper to taste
¼ cup yogurt

Better for you than a trip to the health food store. And cheaper. And tastier.

Method:

1) In a soup pot over low heat, melt butter, then add onions, garlic, and ginger. Stir and cook covered for about 15 minutes, or until onions go soft.

2) When onions are cooked, add stock, prepared carrots, and apples. Bring to a rolling boil.

3) Reduce heat to medium-low and cook, partially covered, for about 20 minutes, or until carrots are cooked through.

4) Pour the soup through a colander, catching the liquid in a large bowl underneath. Using a hand blender, puree the solid ingredients in the pot, gradually adding the soup liquid until mixture becomes thick and smooth.

5) Put pot back on low heat and add orange juice until soup reaches the desired consistency. You may use less than the two cups of OJ, then again, you may use a bit more. Season with salt and pepper. Stir and taste.

To Serve:

Dish out a couple of ladles per bowl and garnish with a dollop of thick yogurt in the middle. Serve with multigrain rolls for enthusiastic dippers.

Can I do anything else for you? Back rubs cost.

A CLOCKWORK ORANGE: Simply put, until you've seen this movie, I don't want to know you. An ultraviolent sci-fi thriller in which a gang of unruly teens terrorize any poor sap that happens to cross their path. For refreshment, the "droogs" head over to a modern-chic bar, where they imbibe a milky liquid that is their drug. Dir: Stanley Kubrick. C: Malcolm McDowell, Patrick Magee, Adrienne Corri. 1971; 137 m.

PULP FICTION: This film is so good that Quentin Tarantino has been able to coast on its laurels for three years and counting. It also resurrected John Travolta's career (check out the diner scene where he gets to dance again). A perfect patchwork of druggies, gangsters, and petty thieves collide in an outrageously daring, violent comedy. Or is it a drama? Or is it a crime flick? Perhaps even horror? Let's just say, my mom hated it. Then again, my dad loved it. Dir: Quentin Tarantino. C: John Travolta, Uma Thurman, Samuel L. Jackson, Bruce Willis. 1994; 160 m.

JUICE: This isn't the kind of juice you'll be wanting to serve the kids at breakfast, or the kind that got charged with murder. It's an unsentimental look at the lives of a group of inner city kids, who get swept into the Harlem crime scene. The natural acting by newcomers, coupled with the unflinching story, is often tough to watch, but that's what makes it great. Dir: Ernest R. Dickerson. C: Omar Epps, Jermaine Hopkins, Khalil Kain, Tupac Shakur. 1992; 96 m.

cantankerou

CRAB AND CORN SOUP

Serves 4

Ingredients:

3 cups chicken stock
14 oz. can creamed corn
2 tbsp. cold water
1 tbsp. cornstarch
¼ tsp. salt
¼ tsp. pepper
½ tsp. sesame oil
¼ cup frozen sweet peas
7 ½ oz. can crab meat, drained and flaked
1 green onion, sliced (for garnish)

Allow me this indulgence: When we were little and my family used to go out and corn soup. But, for some reason, nobody else wanted it. Since my tummy I rarely got to order it. Baby, it's revenge time.

us corn:

Method:

1) In a medium-sized soup pot on high heat, bring stock to a boil and stir in creamed corn. Lower to a simmer.

2) In a small dish, mix together water and cornstarch. Stir into broth, then add salt and pepper, sesame oil, peas, and flaked crab. Let simmer for several more minutes.

To Serve:

Ladle it out and sprinkle with sliced onion. People may want to grab the recipe off of you, but when they ask, just give them a wink and say, "Ancient Chinese secret."

for Chinese food, I always wanted to order the crab was too little to finish a bowl by myself,

BLADE RUNNER: Futuristic L.A. has a high-tech Tokyo look to it, as lawman Harrison Ford slurps down some Asian chow before he learns about his latest mission: to search for and destroy the humanlike androids who have escaped into the general population. A sci-fi classic from Philip K. Dick's novel. Dir: Ridley Scott. C: Harrison Ford, Rutger Hauer, Sean Young, Edward James Olmos, Daryl Hannah. 1982; 122 m.

FIVE EASY PIECES: There is a famous scene in this drama, involving Jack Nicholson trying to make a simple order at a diner. You've definitely heard the shtick before but probably didn't realize it came from this compelling classic about a musician who gives up on his dreams to go work on an oil rig. And the soup? It's so easy to prepare, it has about five pieces! Dir: Bob Rafelson. C: Jack Nicholson, Karen Black, Susan Anspack, Sally Struthers, Lois Smith. 1970; 98 m.

THE KING OF COMEDY: An incredibly unusual comedy that matches the unexpected taste of this soup. Superior performances all around, as daft aspiring comedian Robert De Niro kidnaps late-show host Jerry Lewis, hoping for a go at celebrity. Dir: Martin Scorsese. C: Robert De Niro, Jerry Lewis, Sandra Bernhard. 1983; 109 m.

BLACK AND WHITE BEAN SOUP

Serves 4

Ingredients:

1 tbsp. olive oil
2 small onions, chopped
2 cloves garlic, minced
19 oz. can black beans, rinsed and drained
19 oz. can navy beans (they're actually white),
rinsed and drained
3 cups chicken stock
2 tsp. cumin
½ tsp. salt
½ tsp. black pepper
1 large carrot, grated
1 tbsp. red onion, minced
½ lime, juiced

The yin and yang of the soup world, half of each bowl is filled with a health then topped with lime-drenched carrot shavings. Why can't we all get along

vory:

Method:

1) In 2 medium-sized saucepans, heat ½ tbsp. oil, then add 1 chopped onion and 1 garlic clove to each pot. Stir around for several minutes, until onion is soft.

2) Add the drained can of black beans to one pot and the can of navy beans to the other. Then to each pot add 1 ½ cups of stock, 1 tsp. cumin, and ¼ tsp. salt and pepper. Simmer over low heat for 20 minutes.

3) To prepare salsa, mix grated carrots, red onion, and lime juice together in a small bowl. Season with a bit of the remaining salt and pepper.

To Serve:

Both soups should be equally thick. If one is thinner than the other, add more stock to the thicker one and cook for another few minutes. Then, pour equal amounts of soup into either side of each soup bowl, simultaneously. This takes concentration. Top with a tbsp. of the carrot salsa.

ful ladle of white bean soup and black bean soup, this well?

DO THE RIGHT THING: A disturbing, yet stylishly filmed modern drama about interracial tensions between the Italian owners of a pizza shop, the Korean owners of a variety store, and the African-Americans who reside in a Brooklyn neighborhood. A provocative and explosive picture that predates the Los Angeles riots. Spike Lee was on to something here. Dir: Spike Lee. C: Danny Aiello, Spike Lee, Ossie Davis, Ruby Dee, John Turturro, Rosie Perez. 1989; 120 m.

GUESS WHO'S COMING TO DINNER: Upper crust white-bred woman becomes engaged to black man and invites him home to meet the folks. This fairly tame look at race relations in the '60s would be a nice accompaniment to your own interracial dinner party! Or a cool way of breaking the big news to your parents! Dir: Stanley Kramer. C: Spencer Tracy, Katharine Hepburn, Sidney Poitier, Katherine Houghton. 1967; 108 m.

SIX DEGREES OF SEPARATION: Is there anything that Will Smith can't do? Here he plays a charlatan who poses as the son of Sidney Poitier (see Guess Who's Coming To Dinner) as a way of gaining access into New York City society life. But once he is found out, there are some hard truths to be faced by everyone. From the John Guare play. Dir: Fred Schepisi. C: Stockard Channing, Donald Sutherland, Will Smith. 1993; 112 m.

BROCCOLI CHEDDAR SOUP
Serves 4

Ingredients:

2 tbsp. butter
2 medium onions, chopped
2 garlic cloves, minced
2 heads broccoli (lower part of stems and leaves cut off), roughly chopped
2 carrots, peeled and chopped
1 small potato, peeled and chopped
½ tsp. salt
½ tsp. black pepper
4 cups chicken stock
1 cup table cream (18%)
3 cups cheddar cheese, grated (¼ cup reserved for garnish)

YOU MAY HAVE TO SAUTÉ THE VEGETABLES IN TWO BATCHES.

Ever had one of those days when it feels like the whole world's against you? Have soup. It makes the hurt go away.

Method:

1) In a large frying pan, heat butter over medium, fry onion and garlic for several minutes, then add chopped broccoli, carrots, potato, salt, and pepper. Cook for 10 more minutes, stirring often.

2) In a large soup pot, bring chicken stock to a boil, add cooked vegetables, cover, and cook on medium-low heat for half an hour. Then get out the old hand blender and puree.

3) Taste for salt and pepper, add more if necessary, and remove from heat. Stir in cream and cheese, then heat on low for 5 minutes. Do not let it boil.

To Serve:

Each steaming bowlful is topped with a sprinkling of cheese. Then sit there for a few minutes, watching the cheese melt. A truly meditative experience.

You hate everyone, and they hate you right back.

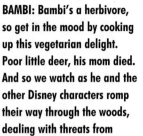

BAMBI: Bambi's a herbivore, so get in the mood by cooking up this vegetarian delight. Poor little deer, his mom died. And so we watch as he and the other Disney characters romp their way through the woods, dealing with threats from predators and natural elements along the way. One of the first animated classics. Dir: David Hand. 1942; 69 m.

TABLE FOR FIVE: Estranged dad (Jon Voight) wants to make amends with his offspring, so off they go on a Mediterranean cruise. Geez, I wish I was mad at my dad. A solid story with excellent acting puts this head and shoulders above typical After School Special fare. A good film for family viewing, but no movie-watching for the kids until they finish their broccoli. Dir: Robert Lieberman. C: Jon Voight, Richard Crenna, Marie-Christine Barrault. 1983; 122 m.

TWIST: We've all done it, even if it was just an accidental off-shoot of slipping on a banana peel. No, I'm not talking about breaking a hip, I'm talking about dancing the twist. Like the soup, this Canadian-made documentary is wonderfully pieced together with humor, grace, and an obvious love for the subject matter/vegetable. Dir: Ron Mann. 1992; 78 m.

thai one on:

COCONUT-CHICKEN SOUP
Serves 6

Ingredients:

14 oz. can unsweetened coconut milk
2 cups chicken stock
14 oz. can straw mushrooms, rinsed and drained
14 oz. can baby corns, rinsed and drained
14 oz. can sliced water chestnuts, drained
2 large boneless, skinless chicken breasts, thinly sliced
2 stalks lemon grass, each chopped into 4 pieces*
1 tbsp. fresh ginger, peeled and minced
1 tbsp. sugar
6 to 8 shakes Tabasco sauce
2 small limes, juiced
¼ cup fresh cilantro, roughly chopped

*Lemon grass looks like long, really thick, woody pieces of grass. It's available in the produce section at Asian markets.

**Memories of a busy Bangkok street come flooding back when I slurp down t
annoying German guy. Still, with the fire of spice in the smooth, soothing b**

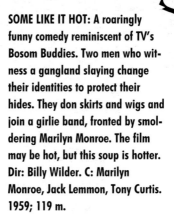

Method:

1) In a large soup pot, combine everything but the lime juice and cilantro. Bring to a boil, making sure it doesn't boil over, then reduce heat to medium for about 5 minutes, or until the chicken is cooked.

2) Take off the heat, mix in the fresh lime juice, give a stir, and taste for seasonings. If you want it spicier, add more Tabasco. If it tastes too tart, add more sugar.

To Serve:

Take the time to fish the lemon grass pieces out of the bowls of soup. They're pretty tough and don't make for good eating. Then top each bowl with chopped cilantro right before serving. An authentic taste of the Far East, without all the soot up your nose.

s trip to exotica. So does the thought of a very th, this soup heats up two ways.

SOME LIKE IT HOT: A roaringly funny comedy reminiscent of TV's Bosom Buddies. Two men who witness a gangland slaying change their identities to protect their hides. They don skirts and wigs and join a girlie band, fronted by smoldering Marilyn Monroe. The film may be hot, but this soup is hotter. Dir: Billy Wilder. C: Marilyn Monroe, Jack Lemmon, Tony Curtis. 1959; 119 m.

APOCALYPSE NOW: Francis Ford Coppola's masterful Vietnam War epic, based on Joseph Conrad's Heart of Darkness, is at once heart-pounding and gut-wrenching. It follows Captain Willard (Martin Sheen) on his journey to meet the maddened officer Kurtz. But who is really the crazy one here? Dish up a whole South East Asian menu, complete with this soup, mango salad, rice, and cashew chicken. Dir: Francis Ford Coppola. C: Marlon Brando, Martin Sheen, Robert Duvall. 1979; 153 m.

EXOTICA: Sexy and sophisticated, this Canadian steamer wowed them at Cannes. Mild-mannered man frequents strip club where woman-child stripper is conscripted to fill the gaping emotional hole in his heart. More about complicated relationships than sex, the film is stylishly beguiling. Spicy food + spicy film = hot night. Dir: Atom Egoyan. C: Bruce Greenwood, Mia Kirshner, Don McKellar. 1995; 104 m.

Body Boost: Carrot-Orange-Ginger Soup, page 66

ICY GAZPACHO
Serves 2

Ingredients:

2 cups V8 juice
2 tbsp. balsamic vinegar
1 sweet red pepper, cored and finely chopped
½ cup English cucumber, finely chopped
1 tomato, cored and finely chopped
¼ cup red onion, finely chopped
1 tsp. sugar
3 shakes Tabasco sauce
1 tbsp. snipped chives (optional)

SOME PEOPLE PREFER THIS SOUP CHUNKLESS. IF YOU COUNT YOURSELF AMONG THEM, PUT A HAND BLENDER IN THE FINISHED SOUP AND PUREE BEFORE CHILLING.

Crunchy, nonfat, and zippy. This super soup is perfect for those sweltering su yourself off the lounge furniture (or the plastic couch).

up is cold:

Method:

1) Combine all of the ingredients (except chives) in a bowl, stir well, cover, and chill in the refrigerator for at least 3 hours.

To Serve:

Ladle the cold soup into big bowls and top with chives (some people like it with croutons). Side it up with some nacho chips and guacamole. Olé.

mmertime lunches when you can't seem to peel

BARCELONA: So, you're living in Spain, having a great time, eating gazpacho for lunch almost every day, and then your idiot brother comes to visit. And you find out your girlfriend is cheating on you. And things start to turn sour at work. If this is your life, you have a lot in common with the protagonist of this quirky comedy. Dir: Whit Stillman. C: Taylor Nichols, Christopher Eigeman, Tushka Bergen, Mira Sorvino. 1994; 101 m.

BELLE EPOQUE: A young, studly army deserter in 1930s Spain is taken in by a loony old man with 4 lovely daughters. The lucky lad has his way with each of them in this sex comedy that won the Oscar for best foreign film. Dir: Fernando Trueba. C: Jorge Sanz, Fernando Fernan Gomez, Maribel Verdu, Ariadna Gil, Miriam Diaz-Aroca, Penelope Cruz. 1992; 108 m.

THE SPANISH GARDENER: A moving drama about a stiff British diplomat living in Spain, who grows to envy the blossoming relationship between his son and the hired help. Based on the A. J. Cronin novel, the movie is as beautifully acted as it is filmed. Dir: Philip Leacock. C: Dirk Bogarde, Maureen Swanson, Jon Whiteley, Cyril Cusack. 1956; 95 m.

courtesy of Scott Burke

salads

BERRY CAESAR
Serves 4

Ingredients:

2 tbsp. olive oil
3 garlic cloves, 1 crushed + 2 chopped
5 slices French bread, cut into ½-inch cubes
¼ tsp. salt (plus a few shakes for the croutons)
1 tsp. Worcestershire sauce
1 egg yolk
¼ tsp. pepper
¼ tsp. sugar
2 tbsp. fresh raspberries
⅛ tsp. mustard powder
1 tbsp. fresh lemon juice
⅓ cup olive oil
1 large head romaine lettuce, washed, dried, and ripped into bite-sized pieces
1 cup fresh seasonal berries (raspberries, blueberries, strawberries, blackberries)
½ cup grated Parmesan cheese

The perennial favorite gets a fun stab in the back with a pink, raspberry-inf berries...then fall, Eater.

erry?

Method:

1) To prepare the croutons, heat 2 tbsp. olive oil in a medium-sized frying pan over medium heat. Add the crushed garlic clove and cook until golden. Remove and trash the clove. Then add the cubed bread, stirring in oil until coated and golden brown. Remove croutons, drain on paper towel, and sprinkle with a few shakes of salt.

2) To make the dressing, use a blender to mix the Worcestershire sauce with garlic, egg yolk, salt, pepper, sugar, 2 tbsp. of raspberries, mustard powder, and lemon juice. Then gradually pour in ⅓ cup of olive oil. Blend until combined.

To Serve:

To a large bowl, add the prepared lettuce, then toss well with enough dressing to coat. Add fresh berries, croutons, and Parmesan cheese. Mix it up and dish it out.

sed dressing, fresh garlic croutons, and seasonal

CESAR AND ROSALIE: A sexy flick about a liberal love triangle that only the French could dream up. A middle-aged woman who has grown bored with her live-in lover, takes on a new, younger companion. But things get really tossed up when her lovers have an affair of their own. Dir: Claude Sautet. C: Yves Montand, Romy Schneider, Sami Frey, Isabelle Huppert. 1972; 110 m.

A DAY IN THE COUNTRY: A stunning work that lavishly winds its way through a family's summertime excursion to the French countryside. In separate conquests, mother and daughter get lucky with male suitors. Ah, the salad days. Dir: Jean Renoir. C: Jean Renoir, Sylvia Bataille, Georges Saint-Saens, Jacques Borel. 1936; 40 m.

JULIUS CAESAR: You can say what you will about Marlon Brando, but he does a mean Caesar — and now so can you. This is one of Hollywood's best mountings of Shakespeare's tale about a bloody power struggle in ancient Rome. Dir: Joseph L. Mankiewicz. C: Louis Calhern, Marlon Brando, James Mason, John Gielgud. 1953; 120 m.

Et Tu, Raspberry? Berry Caesar, page 82

beet generat

RUSSIAN POTATO SALAD
Serves 4

Ingredients:

3 medium potatoes, peeled and quartered
2 eggs
salt and pepper to taste
1 cup bottled baby beets, rinsed and chopped
2 dill pickles, chopped
2 green onion, chopped
2 tbsp. mayonnaise
½ tsp. paprika

Rumor has it that before the old Rusky Gorby hit the road, he used to love th his big melon. Colorful and tasty. The salad, that is.

tion:

Method:

1) Put prepared potatoes in a medium-sized pot, cover with salted water, and boil (partially covered) for 15 minutes or until fork-tender. After 5 minutes of cooking, gently add the eggs to the potato pot. When time's up (or the potatoes are cooked), drain in a colander and chop potatoes into bite-sized pieces. Place in a bowl.

2) Run eggs under cold water, peel, and slice into wedges.

3) In a medium bowl, combine all of the ingredients and stir well. Season with salt and pepper to taste, then refrigerate for several hours before serving.

To Serve:

Gather your comrades together and screw open a bottle of vodka. And I guess sandwiches are a good idea too.

is salad. Pretty much explains the purple stain on

FROM RUSSIA WITH LOVE: Potato salad, Russian potato salad. It may not be the regular leggy dish for James Bond, but it too will undoubtedly be gone by the end of the movie. In this taut thriller, 007 (Sean Connery) accompanies a buxom Russian defector who holds a top-secret code machine. Alas, it's all a devious trap, perpetrated by the evil SPECTRE. Dir: Terence Young. C: Sean Connery, Daniela Bianchi, Lotte Lenya. 1963; 118 m.

THE BATTLESHIP POTEMKIN: A landmark, silent classic. Director Sergei Eisenstein hauntingly illustrates the mutiny on a Russian battleship and its horrifying aftermath during the Revolution of 1905. One of the greatest film moments of all time is the massacre on the Odessa Steps; often imitated, never duplicated. You better finish eating before the film, as this is some serious viewing. Dir: Sergei Eisenstein. C: Alexander Antonov, Vladimir Barsky. Silent; 1925; 65 m.

BURNT BY THE SUN: An Oscar winner for best foreign film, it explores Stalinist Russia as it clutches the summer home of a retired army officer and hero of the Revolution. A breathy story of love and betrayal that'll go great with your honey and a dark room. Dir: Nikita Mikhalkov. C: Nikita Mikhalkov, Oleg Menshikov, Ingeborga Dapkunaite, Nadia Mikhalkov. 1994; 143 m.

SALADE NICOISE
Serves 4

Ingredients:

1 lb. red potatoes (about 4 small ones), washed and cut in half
2 large eggs
½ lb. fresh green beans, tipped at both ends and cut in half
½ tsp. salt
6.5 oz. tin chunk white tuna (packed in water), drained
½ tbsp. sesame oil
2 tbsp. red wine vinegar
1 tsp. Dijon mustard
1 tsp. anchovy paste (optional because
they freak out a lot of people)
1 clove garlic, minced
a pinch of salt and pepper
¼ cup olive oil
1 small head romaine lettuce, washed and dried
2 green onions, washed and dried
½ cup cherry tomatoes, washed and dried
¼ cup pitted black olives
4 anchovies (optional again because of the freaking out thing)
2 tbsp. fresh, chopped parsley

All right, so they tend to be snobby, a little arrogant, and maybe too romantic, but damn it man, they make a good salad. Worth the trouble – although it's not a lot of trouble.

nnection:

Method:

1) Boil prepared potatoes in a pot of unsalted water for 20 minutes. At the 10-minute mark, carefully put the eggs in with the potatoes and boil for 10 minutes. At the 15-minute mark, with just 5 minutes to go, drop in the green beans. When the timer buzzes, drain everything in a large colander, remove the potatoes, and rinse the beans and eggs under cool water.

2) Peel the eggs and cut lengthwise into quarters. Set aside.

3) Take the drained potatoes, sprinkle with a ½ tsp. of salt, and cut into bite-sized pieces. Set aside.

4) In a small bowl, break up the tuna into chunks and toss with the sesame oil.

5) To make the dressing, using a small bowl and whisk, or a hand blender, mix together the vinegar, mustard, anchovy paste, garlic, and salt and pepper. Slowly add the olive oil until everything is well blended.

To Serve:

Line salad plates with several small lettuce leaves, arrange potatoes in the middle, sprinkle with green onions, and artfully add the tomatoes, beans, tuna chunks, and olives. Pour dressing on top and garnish each plate with 2 egg wedges, an anchovy fillet, and a sprinkle of parsley. Bon appétit!

AU REVOIR, LES ENFANTS: Based on filmmaker Louis Malle's childhood in Nazi-occupied France, this French film follows the story of a young boy who suddenly arrives at a rural Catholic boarding school. Friendships emerge as the rich story winds its way to its inevitable conclusion. Dir: Louis Malle. C: Gaspard Manesse, Raphael Fejto, Francine Racette. 1987; 103 m.

HARD-BOILED: A beautifully stylized film in the rich tradition of John Woo. Surprisingly, it's not about eggs, rather, it follows action stars Tony Leung and Chow Yun-Fat as they kick, chop, and blow their way through action sequence after action sequence. Dir: John Woo. C: Chow Yun-fat, Tony Leung, Teresa Mo. 1992; 126 m.

THE FRENCH CONNECTION: Oscar pick for best picture, this action-packed thriller traces rough-around-the-edges New York cop Gene Hackman as he and partner Roy Scheider try to stem the flow of heroin in from France. And hold on to your seats during the breathtaking chase scene at the end. Dir: William Friedkin. C: Gene Hackman, Fernando Rey, Roy Scheider. 1971; 104 m.

SPINACH WITH CANDIED ALMONDS AND MANDARINS

Serves 4

Ingredients:

3 tsp. sugar for coating almonds, plus ½ cup sugar for dressing
1 cup whole almonds
1 bunch fresh spinach
1 tsp. dry mustard
1 tsp. salt
⅓ cup balsamic vinegar
½ cup red onion, minced
2 tbsp. poppy seeds
⅔ cup vegetable oil
10 oz. can mandarin orange sections, drained

More like a trip to the candy store than a healthy salad, the sugared almon dressing will undoubtedly unearth hidden cravings.

alad:

Method:

1) In a small frying pan on medium, heat up 3 tsp. of sugar, add the almonds, and stir around until coated. Watch carefully because they burn easily. Lay out on a cookie sheet to cool, making sure they don't stick together.

2) Wash spinach well and remove stems. Then dry leaves and set aside.

3) Using a hand blender make dressing by combining ½ cup of sugar with mustard, salt, vinegar, minced onion, and poppy seeds. Then gradually add the oil.

4) Add the prepared spinach to a large salad bowl and pour in enough dressing to coat. Mix in cooled candied almonds and mandarins, then toss it all up.

To Serve:

Refined salad seeks simple side plate with rugged outlook on life. Good taste a must.

s, sweet mandarin sections, and cloying poppy seed

WHAT WOULD YOU SAY TO SOME SPINACH? Yuck it up with this Czechoslovakian treat about a zany scientist who invents an antiaging machine. Unfortunately, there are side effects – and eating spinach can cause a whopper! Dir: Vaclav Vorlicek, Milos Makourek. C: Vladimir Mensik, Jiri Sovak. 1976; 90 m.

WHO IS KILLING THE GREAT CHEFS OF EUROPE? A toothsome whodunit about a junk food don who chases his wife through Europe, while gourmet chefs do nosedives into their soup bowls. Have extra salad standing by for any guests who eat like the hilariously gluttonous diner (Robert Morley). Dir: Ted Kotcheff. C: George Segal, Jacqueline Bisset, Robert Morton. 1978; 112 m.

EATING: An insightful comedy in which a group of women gather for a birthday party, and the focus of the conversation turns to food: the good, the bad, and the portion size. I'll tell you, this salad wouldn't last long at that party. Dir: Henry Jaglom. C: Frances Bergen, Lisa Richards, Nelly Alard, Mary Crosby. 1990; 110 m.

We'll Always Have Paris: Roasted Vegetable and Chèvre Salad, page 100

far-out: MARINATED MUSHROOM SALAD
Serves 4

Ingredients:

1 lemon, juiced
1 tbsp. Dijon mustard (cannot be substituted for another type of mustard)
2 garlic cloves, minced
3 tbsp. fresh parsley, minced (1 tbsp. reserved for the garnish)
½ tsp. dried oregano
pinch of salt and pepper
⅓ cup olive oil
1 lb. fresh mushrooms, cleaned and quartered
1 head Bibb lettuce

IT'S A GOOD IDEA TO POLL GUESTS ON LIKES, DISLIKES, AND FOOD ALLERGIES BEFORE MAKING UP THE MENU FOR A DINNER PARTY BECAUSE SERVING STEWED PORK TO A GROUP OF YOUR MUSLIM PALS DURING RAMADAN WON'T GO OVER TOO WELL.

Mushrooms are one of those foods that people either love or hate. You know years later, go into orgasms over the very same item? Weird how that happe

Method:

1) In a medium-sized bowl, whisk together lemon juice, Dijon mustard, garlic, 2 tbsp. of the parsley, oregano, and salt and pepper.

2) Then, slowly but surely, trickle in the olive oil, whisking constantly until a thickish dressing emerges.

3) Toss prepared mushrooms with dressing until well coated. Cover and refrigerate for several hours.

To Serve:

Line salad plates with a few leaves of washed and dried lettuce. Place equal portions of marinated mushrooms on top, and scatter with the remaining tbsp. of fresh parsley.

how sometimes you can detest something, and then ns in relationships...I mean foods.

IF YOU COULD ONLY COOK: Even if you can't cook, you can prepare this zesty mushroom salad. As for the entertainment, it's a screwball comedy in which a wealthy man and a dirt-poor woman go undercover as servants to a mob family. Dir: William A. Seiter. C: Herbert Marshall, Jean Arthur, Leo Carrillo, Lionel Stander. 1935; 70 m.

SHORT CUTS: A brilliant feat by director Robert Altman, as he intertwines the seemingly separate lives of a host of Southern California families, from Raymond Carver's short stories. It's a bit off the beaten track, and sometimes difficult to watch, but it's unlike anything you've seen before. Dir: Robert Altman. C: Tim Robbins, Julianne Moore, Anne Archer, Matthew Modine, Lily Tomlin, Lyle Lovett. 1993; 189 m.

SLACKER: Just because you're a big old lazy bones doesn't mean you can't eat tasty food! Make this dish, and in no time, you'll be eating a gourmet salad. Then you can slouch back down in front of the tube and watch this blithe comedy about a group of aimless Austin, Texans, who ramble on about diverse, and often hilarious, subjects. The cast of non-professionals are as charming as they come. Dir: Richard Linklater. 1991; 97 m.

eggo my ma

MANGO
SALAD
Serves 4

Ingredients:

2 ripe mangoes, peeled and sliced
1 green pepper, cored and sliced
2 red peppers, cored and sliced
3 small limes, juiced
1 tbsp. sugar
1 tbsp. vegetable oil
1 clove garlic, minced
½ tsp. chili flakes
1 tbsp. chopped peanuts (optional)
1 tbsp. chopped fresh coriander (optional)
1 head romaine lettuce, leaves washed and dried

You're a rebel, you break the rules, you mix fruit and vegetables and sugar of the harvest; you are free.

96

ngo:

Method:

1) Peel and slice mangoes into long thin strips. Set aside in a medium-sized bowl. Cut the core out of the peppers, remove all seeds, and slice in long, thin pieces like the mangoes. Add to mango bowl.

2) Cut the 3 limes in half and squeeze the juice out of the 6 halves into a small bowl. Add the sugar, oil, garlic, and chili flakes. Mix together until the sugar dissolves, then pour over the bowl of sliced mangoes and peppers. Toss together until everything is coated in dressing.

To Serve:

Sprinkle the chopped peanuts and coriander over the salad, then dish portions onto plates lined with clean leaves of crisp romaine lettuce.

nd spice. You have unleashed the forbidden dance

SCENT OF GREEN PAPAYA: A poignant Vietnamese drama that smells like a winner. Young house servant falls in love with young master in 1950s Saigon. Lustily made and fancifully acted. Mango salad and Pad Thai do nicely for a quick bite. Dir: Tran Anh Hung. C: Tran Nu Yen-Khe, Lu Man San, Truong Thi Loc. 1994; 104 m.

GOOD MORNING, VIETNAM: Comedian-turned-thespian Robin Williams shines as motor-mouthed Saigon disc jockey, Adrian Cronauer. His job was to entertain homesick soldiers by turning the tunes, but it was his sharp-tongued monologues that really got the troops fired up. Dir: Barry Levinson. C: Robin Williams, Forest Whitaker, Bruno Kirby, Robert Wuhl. 1988; 121 m.

THE KILLING FIELDS: The film is based on the real-life experiences of New York Times correspondent Sidney Schanberg during the rise of Pol Pot, and the friendship he forges with his guide Dith Pran. After surviving the horrors of war-torn Cambodia, Oscar winner Haing S. Ngor was murdered on his driveway in L.A. And that just sucks. Dir: Roland Joffe. C: Sam Waterston, Haing S. Ngor, John Malkovich. 1984; 142 m.

sacred salad

TABBOULEH
Serves 6 to 8

Ingredients:

3 cups vegetable or chicken stock
1 tsp. salt
¼ tsp. chili flakes
1 ½ cups uncooked bulgar wheat
2 large tomatoes, cored and chopped
1 small onion, chopped
1 small cucumber, peeled and chopped
juice of 2 small lemons
2 cloves garlic, minced
2 tbsp. olive oil
1 tbsp. fresh mint leaves, chopped
½ cup fresh parsley, chopped

After a few thousand years of experimentation, our ancestors perfected the Amazing what you dream up while wandering in the desert.

Method:

1) Boil the stock in a medium-sized saucepan, add the salt and chili flakes, then slowly add the bulgar to the bubbling liquid. Cover the pot and take off the heat. Set aside for 1 hour.

2) If you haven't already prepared the vegetables, lemon juice, garlic, oil, and herbs, do so now, and toss together in a medium bowl.

3) When the hour is up, take the lid off the pot, carefully drain away any excess liquid, and chill in your serving bowl, in the fridge.

4) It should be cool within an hour or 2. When thoroughly chilled, throw the veggie mixture into the serving bowl. Toss well.

To Serve:

This salad is best served with other Middle Eastern treats, like hummus and pita, for a yummy starter course or light lunch.

ealthy side dish – this vitamin-packed salad.

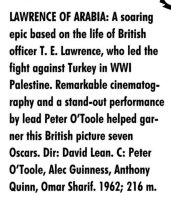

LAWRENCE OF ARABIA: A soaring epic based on the life of British officer T. E. Lawrence, who led the fight against Turkey in WWI Palestine. Remarkable cinematography and a stand-out performance by lead Peter O'Toole helped garner this British picture seven Oscars. Dir: David Lean. C: Peter O'Toole, Alec Guinness, Anthony Quinn, Omar Sharif. 1962; 216 m.

THE TEN COMMANDMENTS: Another really big picture, it's a testament to director Cecil B. DeMille's unflinching vision and artistry. You've probably heard the story before, a little tale about Moses, the Israelites, and their backbreaking journey through the desert for some 40-odd years. The magical parting of the Red Sea is just one of the reasons this won an Oscar for special effects. Dir: Cecil B. DeMille. C: Charlton Heston, Yul Brynner, Anne Baxter, Edward G. Robinson. 1956; 219 m.

RAIDERS OF THE LOST ARK: Still one of the biggest box-office hits of all time. Archaeologist Harrison Ford travels through the Mideast (AKA the taboulleh capital of the world) on a mission to save the lost ark from a band of scheming Nazis. A crazy adventure story that leaves your heart pounding, while being quirkily funny and a treasure to watch. It spawned a popular trilogy. Dir: Steven Spielberg. C: Harrison Ford, Karen Allen, Paul Freeman, Ronald Lacey. 1981; 116 m.

ROASTED VEGETABLE AND CHÈVRE SALAD
Serves 4

Ingredients:

1 tbsp. soy sauce
3 tbsp. olive oil (1 tbsp. reserved for dressing)
1 large eggplant, thinly sliced lengthwise
2 zucchinis, sliced into 1-inch rounds
1 red onion, cut into 1-inch wedges
2 yellow peppers, cored and cut into wedges
2 cups mixed baby greens
2 tbsp. balsamic vinegar
1 garlic clove, minced
salt and pepper to taste
10 oz. goat cheese (chèvre), sliced into 4 even rounds
2 tbsp. fresh basil, chopped

They can't get enough of Camembert, Brie, or Jerry Lewis. I swear, sometime grilled salad, and you'll be labeled anything but.

ave paris:

Method:

1) Heat BBQ (or hibachi) to medium-high heat.

2) Mix soy sauce with two tbsp. of olive oil and brush prepared veggies with the mixture. Then lay vegetables on hot BBQ grill, flipping every so often, for about 7 minutes. Some vegetables cook faster than others, so take cooked vegetables off and set aside in a bowl to cool.

3) Wash and dry baby greens, and toss with vinegar, oil, garlic, salt and pepper. Dish out onto 4 salad plates

4) Wrap each goat cheese round with a slice of eggplant, then place on the dressed greens. Dish grilled veggies out around salad and top with chopped basil and an extra drizzle of oil and balsamic vinegar.

To Serve:

Have a basket of sliced baguette standing by to serve with the salad. And doesn't a nice bottle of white wine sound refreshing?

the French can be so cheesy. Serve this luscious

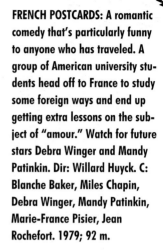

FRENCH POSTCARDS: A romantic comedy that's particularly funny to anyone who has traveled. A group of American university students head off to France to study some foreign ways and end up getting extra lessons on the subject of "amour." Watch for future stars Debra Winger and Mandy Patinkin. Dir: Willard Huyck. C: Blanche Baker, Miles Chapin, Debra Winger, Mandy Patinkin, Marie-France Pisier, Jean Rochefort. 1979; 92 m.

THE TENANT: This horror-filled American/French collaboration stars director Roman Polanski (before he was booted out of the country) as a loser who rents an apartment that was once inhabited by a suicidal man. It's a chilling ride that'll spook the pants off of you. Dir: Roman Polanski. C: Roman Polanski, Isabelle Adjani, Shelley Winters, Melvyn Douglas, Jo Van Fleet. 1976; 125 m.

MY DINNER WITH ANDRE: If the conversation at dinner was always like this, we'd never leave the bloody table! Two men, one an actor/playwright, the other a director, chat about topics ranging from the heady to the trite. By the end of the picture you wish they were your pals because then they'd have to keep on talking. Maybe if you bribed them with some irresistible chèvre? Dir: Louis Malle. C: Andre Gregory, Wallace Shawn. 1981; 110 m.

ye haw!

SOUTHERN SLAW

Serves 4

Ingredients:

½ small red cabbage
½ tsp. salt (plus a few shakes for the cabbage)
1 red pepper
2 small carrots
½ cooking onion
½ cup corn kernels (fresh cooked or thawed frozen)
¼ tsp. garlic powder
⅓ cup sugar
⅓ cup white vinegar
¼ tsp. pepper
1 ½ tbsp. vegetable oil

This shiny, happy coleslaw is great for a picnic or BBQ, with chili or sided up C-O-L-E-S-L-A-W.

Method:

1) Cut the ½ cabbage into several wedges and soak in cold water with a few shakes of salt.

2) Core the pepper and thinly slice; peel the carrots and grate; cut the ½ onion into paper-thin slices; then place the veggies (except corn) in a bowl.

3) Remove cabbage from bowl of salted water and finely shred with a sharp knife. Put in a large bowl and add vegetables.

4) In a small bowl, mix together the ingredients to make the dressing (rest of ingredients, minus the corn), then toss in with cabbage and vegetable mixture. Refrigerate for 24 hours before serving. Throw in corn right before bringing the slaw to the table.

To Serve:

After the day of marinating is up (you obviously have to plan ahead for this dish), dump the coleslaw into a nice serving bowl and top with a bunch of chopped parsley if you like.

with a sandwich. How do you spell versatility?

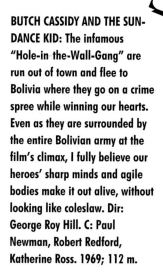

BUTCH CASSIDY AND THE SUNDANCE KID: The infamous "Hole-in-the-Wall-Gang" are run out of town and flee to Bolivia where they go on a crime spree while winning our hearts. Even as they are surrounded by the entire Bolivian army at the film's climax, I fully believe our heroes' sharp minds and agile bodies make it out alive, without looking like coleslaw. Dir: George Roy Hill. C: Paul Newman, Robert Redford, Katherine Ross. 1969; 112 m.

LEGENDS OF THE FALL: When I caught this Western flick in the theaters, there were audible gasps from the audience when hunky Brad Pitt came riding onto the screen. A sweeping epic, full of breathtaking, Oscar-winning cinematography. Dir: Edward Zwick. C: Brad Pitt, Anthony Hopkins, Aidan Quinn, Julia Ormond, Henry Thomas. 1994; 133 m.

SHANE: Many critics rank this as the best Western of all time. A mysterious stranger comes to town and wins the hearts of a group of homesteaders who are at odds with an evil group of cattlemen. Sounds simplistic, but it's not. Dinner, on the other hand, is, if you dish up some easy chili, coleslaw, and corn bread. Dir: George Stevens. C: Alan Ladd, Jean Arthur, Van Heflin, Jack Palance. 1953; 117 m.

mains

retro loaf:
MEATLOAF FOR THE ALTERNATIVE DINER
Serves 6

Ingredients:

(Preheat oven to 350 degrees Fahrenheit)

2 lbs. lean ground beef*
1 egg, beaten
1 ½ cups whole-wheat breadcrumbs
1 cup tomato sauce (¼ cup reserved for topping), bottled or homemade
1 tsp. Worcestershire sauce
½ cup warm water
4 shakes Tabasco sauce
1 packet onion soup mix (single serving)
3 hard-boiled eggs, peeled
vegetable oil spray

*If you're not into red meat, substitute the lean ground beef with ground chicken, ground turkey, or a combination of the two.

How TO BOIL AN EGG. IT MAY SEEM LIKE THE SIMPLEST OF TASKS, BUT WITHOUT THE RIGHT INFORMATION YOUR HARD-BOILEDS MAY GIVE YOU A RAW DEAL. TO BOIL ONE OR MORE EGGS, FILL A SMALL POT WITH WATER AND ADD 1 TSP. OF SALT. BRING TO A ROLLING BOIL AND THEN GENTLY ADD EGGS TO THE WATER. REDUCE HEAT TO A SIMMER. SET A TIMER FOR 12 MINUTES AND LET THE EGGS COOK UNCOVERED. WHEN THE DINGER GOES, YOUR EGGS ARE COOKED. PUT THE POT IN A SINK AND RUN COLD WATER OVER THE EGGS UNTIL THEY COOL. THEN PEEL, RINSE, AND EAT.

Not just a fat singer on a Harley, Meatloaf is th dinner. It's fast, cheap, and with the right meat,

Method:

1) Mix everything together in a large bowl, except for the hard-boiled eggs and ¼ cup tomato sauce.

2) Spray loaf pan with vegetable oil.

3) Pour half of the mixture into the loaf pan, pat it down, and place the peeled, hard-boiled eggs down the middle, end to end.

4) Pour the remaining mixture on top and pat it down, making sure to completely cover the eggs.

5) Top with the remaining ¼ cup tomato sauce.

6) Bake uncovered in the 350 degree Fahrenheit oven for 1 hour.

To Serve:

For a truly retro meal, place a hearty wedge of meatloaf on a big old plate and side it up with mashed potatoes and sweet peas.

stuff to eat when you feel like a home-spun beefy healthy. Paradise by the TV-screen light.

GREASE: You've solved your problems, and you see the light, you've got a hoard of guests, you want to feed them right. Meatloaf's the word. I won a dance contest at my brother's bar mitzvah playing air guitar to "Greased Lightning." This is a wicked, fun film to play for a group because everyone knows the songs, and they can all get up and work off the meal doing the mashed potato. Dir: Randal Kleiser. C: John Travolta, Olivia Newton-John, Stockard Channing. 1978; 110 m.

AMERICAN GRAFFITI: This nostalgic look at small-town America explores the cruising rituals of a bunch of high-school students on the last Friday night after graduation. The rock 'n' roll soundtrack and diner food will make you nostalgic for your parents' glory days. This film was the precursor to the hit TV series Happy Days. Dir: George Lucas. C: Richard Dreyfuss, Ron Howard, Paul LeMat, Cindy Williams. 1973; 110 m.

DINER: The year is 1959; the place, Baltimore. We are invited to watch a clan of college-aged lifelong pals as they're dragged kicking and screaming into adulthood. This comedy is where it all began for the cast of unknowns, and it's also where "Six Degrees of Kevin Bacon" got its start. After your retro dinner, pop up a bowl of corn but don't do what Mickey Rourke did in the infamous date scene. Dir: Barry Levinson. C: Steve Guttenberg, Daniel Stern, Mickey Rourke, Kevin Bacon. 1982; 110 m.

Retro Loaf: Meatloaf for the Alternative Diner, page 106

paranormal

OUT OF THIS WORLD CASHEW CHICKEN

Serves 2

Ingredients:

2 large boneless, skinless chicken breasts, cut into ½-inch cubes
1 tsp. ginger, peeled and minced
1 tbsp. rice wine vinegar
2 tsp. cornstarch
1 tbsp. water
3 tsp. soy sauce (2 tsp. reserved for the sauce)
2 tbsp. vegetable oil
2 stalks celery, sliced
½ can sliced water chestnuts, drained
1 green pepper, cored and chopped
½ tsp. sugar
¼ tsp. sesame oil
3 shakes Tabasco sauce
½ cup salted cashew nuts

What you've got here are plump morsels of chicken coated in a fragrant Orie nuts. The sauce is out there. Trust no one...but me.

food:

Method:

1) Cut chicken into cubes and marinate in ginger, rice wine vinegar, cornstarch, water, and a tsp. of soy sauce. Stir and set aside for 30 minutes.

2) Heat vegetable oil on high in a wok and add meat with marinade. Stir constantly so that chicken pieces don't stick to wok or each other. When chicken turns white, add vegetables and water chestnuts, and stir-fry for 3 minutes. Add the remaining soy sauce, sugar, sesame oil, and Tabasco sauce. Stir-fry for 2 more minutes.

3) If wok is too dry, add a couple tbsp. of water, bring to a boil, and add cashew nuts. Cook 1 more minute.

To Serve:

I like it nice and hot, ladled over steamed rice. But kasha, noodles, and couscous are also good alternatives. If you have any creative ideas of your own, be my guest.

ntal sauce and tossed together with crunchy cashew

THE WEDDING BANQUET: In an attempt to placate his parents, a Taiwanese homosexual groom plans an all-out wedding that gets totally out of hand. The film cleverly makes fun of everyone and everything, without being the least bit offensive. It'll make you hungry, so make loads of food. Dir: Ang Lee. C: Winston Chao, May Chin, Mitchell Lichtenstein, Sihung Lung. 1993; 111 m.

THE BLUE KITE: So true to life, it was banned in its country of origin. The drama follows a young boy and his family as they try to cope with the effects of political upheaval and the Cultural Revolution in China. Mesmerizing performances all around. Dir: Tian Zhuangzhuang. C: Chen Ziaoman, Lu Liping, Pu Quanxin, Li Xuejian. 1994; 138 m.

THE FORTUNE COOKIE: The first of five (and counting) Walter Matthau/Jack Lemmon pairings has Oscar winner Matthau as an ambulance-chasing lawyer who coaxes Lemmon into faking an injury for a big insurance payoff. Funny stuff. Dir: Billy Wilder. C: Jack Lemmon, Walter Matthau, Ron Rich, Cliff Osmond, Judi West. 1966; 125 m.

fisherman's
CIOPPINO SEAFOOD STEW

Serves 2

Ingredients:

1 tbsp. olive oil
2 shallots, chopped
1 garlic clove, minced
1 small green pepper, cored and chopped
1 cup canned tomatoes, drained and chopped
¼ tsp. dried basil
¼ tsp. dried oregano
¼ tsp. paprika
1 cup dry white wine
¾ tsp. sugar
8 fresh large shrimp in their shells, rinsed under cold water
10 fresh mussels, scrubbed under cold water
a 1 lb. cooked lobster
salt and pepper to taste
2 tsp. fresh parsley, chopped
½ lemon, cut into 2 wedges

Taking your partner out for a big seafood dinner says, "I'm spending this ca it up yourself says, "If this turns out well, tonight's the night."

112

fodder:

Method:

1) In a large soup pot, heat oil on medium. Add chopped shallots and garlic, and let cook for a few minutes. Stir in chopped pepper, tomatoes, basil, oregano, and paprika. Cook for another 2 minutes. Add wine and sugar, bring to a boil, reduce heat to medium-low, then add shrimp, mussels, and lobster. Cover and cook for 4 minutes, or until the shrimp have turned pink and the mussels have opened. Discard any mussels that didn't pop open on their own. Season with salt and pepper.

2) Give the stew a big old stir, then fish out the lobster. Remove the claws, give each a whack (so that you'll be able to get at the meat later), then pick the lobster meat out of the body and tail, letting the juices fall into the stew, and add to the pot. Cook for 1 more minute. Reserve the lobster's head and tail for garnish.

To Serve:

Using the biggest bowls you have (pasta bowls would be primo), dish out the stew, making sure each eater gets a bit of everything. Give one bowl the head, another the tail, and both a meaty claw. Let loose with the fresh chopped parsley and a wedge of lemon for squeezing. Crusty Italian rolls are a must for dipping.

sh on you because I think you're worth it." Cooking

SPLASH: A very funny love affair between man and mermaid. When the finned wonder flip-flops her way into New York to pursue her love interest, the military, and scientist Eugene Levy, try to get their hands on her, leading to fishy business. Watch for mermaid Daryl Hannah's whimsical lobster-eating scene. Dir: Ron Howard. C: Daryl Hannah, Tom Hanks, John Candy, Eugene Levy. 1984; 109 m.

ANNIE HALL: Winner of a handful of Oscars, including best picture, this semiautobiographical Woody Allen comedy has him paired with the hat and tie-wearing Diane Keaton as the title character. Fashion trends were set, and cooking up lobster was never the same. Dir: Woody Allen. C: Woody Allen, Diane Keaton, Tony Roberts. 1977; 94 m.

JAWS: This is the most suspense-filled movie you will likely ever see. Na na. Na na. Na na, na na, na na, na na. Thankfully I've always been surrounded by freshwater lakes, otherwise the summers would have been mighty unbearable with no place to cool my heels. Dir: Steven Spielberg. C: Roy Scheider, Robert Shaw, Richard Dreyfuss. 1975; 124 m.

SPICY INDIAN DAL
Serves 2

Ingredients:

1 cup red lentils
3 cups water
½ tsp. salt
2 cooking onions, chopped
4 medium tomatoes or 8 canned plum tomatoes
1 tbsp. vegetable oil
1 tsp. garlic powder
1 tbsp. cumin
1 tbsp. curry
½ tsp. cayenne pepper
1 tbsp. cashews (toasted)
2 cups rice, cooked

Method:

1) Pour dry lentils in a shallow bowl and pick through them, discarding any tiny stones, sticks, or discolored lentils.

2) In a medium-sized saucepan, bring water with the salt to a rolling boil. Add the lentils, stir, and cover.

RICE COMES IN A VARIETY OF FORMS, THE MOST COMMON BEING WHITE, LONG-GRAIN, SHORT-GRAIN, BROWN, AND BASMATI. THE BEST WAY TO COOK LONG-GRAIN IS TO BRING WATER TO A ROLLING BOIL, SO THAT THE GRAINS DON'T STICK TOGETHER. LONG-GRAIN RICE, BOILED IN A MEDIUM-SIZED POT, WILL TAKE ABOUT 11 MINUTES TO COOK. THE RICE IS PERFECTLY COOKED WHEN THE GRAINS, SMOOSHED BETWEEN YOUR THUMB AND INDEX FINGER, MASH INTO A FIRM PASTE. GENERALLY, 1 CUP OF RICE + 2 CUPS WATER = 3 CUPS COOKED RICE.

Too broke to go to India, but still want to discover the mystery? With five bu you can at least eat like him. After dinner, send a postcard.

ret:

3) Chop the onion, then core and chop the tomatoes.

4) To a large frying pan, add the oil, heat on medium-high, then toss in the chopped onion. Cook, stirring every so often, until the onions begin to soften. Add the tomatoes, stir together, then add the spices and stir again. Reduce to medium heat and cook for 5 minutes.

5) Carefully pour the cooked vegetable mixture into the pot of cooking lentils. Stir together, adding more water if the mixture looks good enough to eat, but the lentils aren't fully cooked yet.

6) Continue cooking dal on low heat for 20 minutes, covered, until it's nice and thick. The total cooking time will be 30 to 40 minutes.

7) Taste for seasonings. If not spicy enough add more cayenne or some chili flakes. If adding more spices, cook dal for another minute to allow the flavors to meld.

To Serve:

Spoon a couple of ladles over rice (long-grain, brown, or even the instant stuff, like Minute Rice). Top with toasted cashews.

ks and half an hour you can't become Gandhi, but

GANDHI: An exquisite film biography that chronicles the life and rise to power of the great Indian leader, who headed the campaign for the independence of India after WW II. The vastness of this picture (which included thousands of extras) doesn't detract from its intimate feeling. It garnered a whopping two fistfuls of Oscars. And even though Gandhi didn't eat much, doesn't mean your guests won't go for a full on Indian feast. Do it up and do it right. Dir: Richard Attenborough. C: Ben Kingsley, Candice Bergen, Edward Fox, John Gielgud, Martin Sheen. 1982; 188 m.

A PASSAGE TO INDIA: Based on the novel by E. M. Forster, the film starts out as a romantic adventure, in which a British woman has a personal awakening in 1920s India. But then the film takes a serious turn, and we find ourselves witnessing a dramatic court case centered around an attempted rape. It too won some well-deserved Oscars. Dir: David Lean. C: Judy Davis, Victor Banerjee, Alec Guinness, Peggy Ashcroft. 1984; 163 m.

SALAAM BOMBAY! A young Indian boy learns the hard truths about life on the mean streets of Bombay, as assorted criminals and prostitutes educate him on the finer points of poverty during this sobering tour. A visually enthralling film in which director Mira Nair cast real-life street kids as the street kids. Dir: Mira Nair. C: Shafiq Syed, Raghubir Yadav, Aneeta Kanwar, Hansa Vithal. 1988; 113 m.

foxy fromage

CHEESE FONDUE
Serves 4

Ingredients:

2 baguettes
1 ½ cups dry white wine
¾ lb. shredded Gruyère cheese
¾ lb. shredded Emmenthal cheese
1 tsp. cornstarch
1 tbsp. kirsch (if you don't want to invest in a bottle, substitute with 1 tbsp. lemon juice)
pepper to taste

You say you have three hungry friends coming over for dinner, and all you h
out the fondue pot – it's party time! And if you don't have some cheese and w

e:

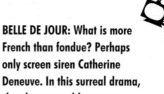

Method:

1) Cut bread into thick slices, then rip each slice into 4 pieces. Each piece should have some crust on it.

2) Pour wine into a heavy saucepan on medium-high heat, and just before the wine boils, add both cheeses and cornstarch. Continuously stir with a wooden spoon, and keep stirring until the cheese is thoroughly melted. Never let the fondue boil. Add kirsch and season with pepper.

3) Put bread cubes in a big basket and set on the dinner table, beside the waiting fondue pot.

To Serve:

Pour fondue mixture into fondue pot and place over the lit burner. Give one more big stir and let everyone go at it with their fondue sticks. Dip, dip, dip.

ave in the fridge is some cheese and wine? Break ine, go buy some. Spend on your friends.

BELLE DE JOUR: What is more French than fondue? Perhaps only screen siren Catherine Deneuve. In this surreal drama, she plays a wealthy woman who goes to work in a classy Paris brothel. Her clients' odd requests, coupled with her own sexual fantasies, are as hot as steaming cheese. Dir: Luis Bunuel. C: Catherine Deneuve, Jean Sorel, Michel Piccoli, Genevieve Page. 1967; 100 m.

LAST TANGO IN PARIS: A gorgeous French drama in which Marlon Brando plays a recently widowed man who falls into an illicit love affair with a young stranger. Quite a groundbreaking film, smoldering and thought provoking, especially during the much talked-about butter scene. Dir: Bernardo Bertolucci. C: Marlon Brando, Maria Schneider, Jean-Pierre Leaud. 1973; 129 m.

THE RED BALLOON: A short, French children's classic. I first saw this at a friend's birthday party when I was in grade one, and I never forgot it. A young boy is followed around Paris by a red balloon, during which time he is taught (without much dialogue) about death and rebirth. The ending is truly a thing of beauty. It'll melt your socks off. Dir: Albert Lamorisse, Robert Enrico. C: Pascal Lamorisse, Roger Jacquet. 1956; 34 m.

a river runs

PAN-FRIED RAINBOW TROUT

Serves 2

Ingredients:

two 8 to 10 oz. rainbow trout or perch
½ tsp. salt
¼ tsp. pepper
¼ cup flour
1 tbsp. olive oil
2 small lemons, 1 juiced, 1 halved for garnish
¼ cup dry white wine
¼ cup fresh chopped parsley
½ cup unsalted butter

Method:

1) With a sharp knife, remove fins from each fish and scrape off any scales that may still be on the skin. Wipe fish clean with a damp paper towel.

WHEN USING NONSTICK PANS, NEVER USE KNIVES, FORKS, OR METAL UTENSILS TO STIR FOOD AROUND. IT DAMAGES THE COATING AND WILL EVENTUALLY TURN YOUR NONSTICKS INTO A STICKY SITUATION.

Listen to the waves and the whine of the fly rod, check out Brad P camping in front of your TV.

skillet:

2) On a large plate, mix salt and pepper in with flour. Roll fish in mixture to coat.

3) In a large nonstick frying pan, heat oil over medium-high heat.

4) Place both fish in the hot pan and cook for 4 minutes on each side (8 minutes total). Nudge the fish a bit while they cook to be sure they're not sticking. Remove from pan and set aside.

5) Scrape out any large fish bits from pan, then over medium heat, add lemon juice, wine, and chopped parsley. Cook for 1 minute, then slowly whisk in butter, a tbsp. at a time, until sauce bubbles and thickens slightly.

6) Plant a fish on each dinner plate and coat with sauce.

To Serve:

Place half a lemon beside each fish and side with some steamed asparagus and Keep Your Eyes On These Guys: Sweet Potato "Fries" (p.30).

tt's bum, make yourself some fresh fish, and go

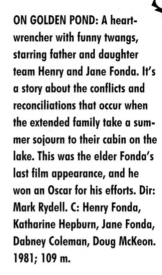

ON GOLDEN POND: A heart-wrencher with funny twangs, starring father and daughter team Henry and Jane Fonda. It's a story about the conflicts and reconciliations that occur when the extended family take a summer sojourn to their cabin on the lake. This was the elder Fonda's last film appearance, and he won an Oscar for his efforts. Dir: Mark Rydell. C: Henry Fonda, Katharine Hepburn, Jane Fonda, Dabney Coleman, Doug McKeon. 1981; 109 m.

RIVER'S EDGE: This isn't teen angst in the John Hughes oeuvre. It's harsh, bold, and as fresh as this fish dish. A group of suburban teens are so world-weary that when their friend points them toward the murdered body of a classmate, they barely react. It's bleak stuff, based on a real-life murder case. Dir: Tim Hunter. C: Crispin Glover, Keanu Reeves, Ione Skye, Daniel Roebuck, Dennis Hopper. 1987; 99 m.

RUMBLE FISH: An innovative drama shot in black and white, with flashes of color. Based on the S. E. Hinton novel, it's the tale of disenchanted youths trying to cope with their dreams and realities. Tropical fish are a magical escape for troubled lead Mickey Rourke. Dir: Francis Ford Coppola. C: Matt Dillon, Mickey Rourke, Diane Lane, Dennis Hopper. 1983; 94 m.

have a cow,

VEAL MARSALA WITH GLAZED CARROTS

Serves 2

Ingredients:

2 veal cutlets, pounded thin
1 cup baby carrots (bite-sized,
prepared carrots that come in cellophane bags)
1 tbsp. butter
2 tsp. sugar
¼ cup flour
¼ tsp. salt
¼ tsp. pepper
¼ tsp. paprika
2 tbsp. olive oil
1 tbsp. + ½ cup Marsala wine
¼ cup sliced mushrooms
salt and pepper to taste

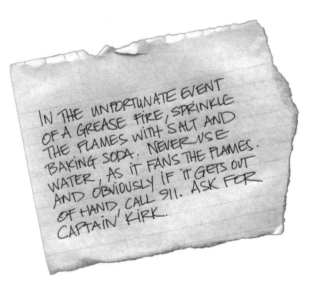

IN THE UNFORTUNATE EVENT OF A GREASE FIRE, SPRINKLE THE FLAMES WITH SALT AND BAKING SODA. NEVER USE WATER, AS IT FANS THE FLAMES. AND OBVIOUSLY IF IT GETS OUT OF HAND, CALL 911. ASK FOR CAPTAIN KIRK.

No, you're not an underachiever. You know how to make a cordon bleu-caliber meal while quoting entire passages from the Bart Simpson oeuvre. Get bent.

man:

Method:

1) Take veal cutlets, put between two sheets of wax paper, and pound thin with a tenderizer or mallet.

2) Put baby carrots in a small pot, add enough water to just cover carrots, then drop in butter and sugar. Cook on high heat, stirring every so often. They should take 10 to 15 minutes to cook.

3) On a plate, mix flour together with salt, pepper, and paprika, then dip each cutlet in the seasoned flour.

4) In a medium-sized pan, heat oil on medium-high, then add the veal plus a tbsp. of Marsala, and cook for 2 minutes on each side. When cooked, remove cutlets (set aside) and add ½ cup Marsala to pan. Bring to a boil and stir in sliced mushrooms. Cook for 1 minute.

5) Check carrots for doneness. If they're cooked but there's still some water in the pot, drain water out and put the carrots back on high heat so that the sugar and butter form a glaze.

To Serve:

Plate up the veal, pour mushroom sauce on top, season with salt and pepper, then side it with glazed carrots and some steamed red potatoes. How delectably colorful.

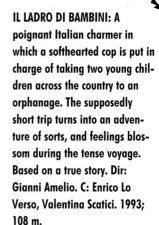

IL LADRO DI BAMBINI: A poignant Italian charmer in which a softhearted cop is put in charge of taking two young children across the country to an orphanage. The supposedly short trip turns into an adventure of sorts, and feelings blossom during the tense voyage. Based on a true story. Dir: Gianni Amelio. C: Enrico Lo Verso, Valentina Scatici. 1993; 108 m.

LA DOLCE VITA: This surrealist journey through Rome follows a society journalist as he meanders his way through the decline of civilization, in a series of vignettes. Federico Fellini's dreamy imprint make this an icon in the film world. Dir: Federico Fellini. C: Marcello Mastroianni, Anouk Aimee, Anita Ekberg, Barbara Steele, Nadia Gray. 1960; 175 m.

THE POSTMAN: An Italian modern-day classic that gained publicity when its star died of heart failure the day after filming was completed. The story revolves around an uneducated village postman and the friendship he forges with an exiled Chilean poet/activist. Through the renowned poet, he learns the value of an education, and political activism, and the importance of love. Dir: Brandon Judell. C: Massimo Troisi, Philippe Noiret, Maria Grazia Cucinotta, Linda Moretti. 1995; 98 m.

the noodle a

PAD THAI
Serves 4

Ingredients:

½ of a 1 lb. rice "stick" noodles package
1 cup bean sprouts (¼ cup reserved for the garnish)
3 green onions, each chopped into 5 pieces (7 pieces reserved for the garnish)
1 red pepper, cored and sliced
3 tbsp. chopped peanuts (½ reserved for the garnish)
2 tbsp. vegetable oil
2 cloves garlic, finely chopped
2 boneless, skinless chicken breasts, cut into strips*
2 large eggs, beaten
4 tbsp. ketchup
2 tbsp. white vinegar
2 tsp. sugar
1 tsp. chili flakes
3 small limes, 2 juiced + 1 quartered for the garnish
1 orange, sliced

*If you're not a meat eater, simply leave the chicken out or substitute with 8 oz. of firm, cubed tofu.

**Probably the most popular of the North Americanized Thai dishes, but you'v
your problems. Just follow this recipe to Thai heaven.**

nd 1:

Method:

1) In a medium-sized pot, boil water, add rice noodles, and cook for 6 minutes. Drain well.

2) Prepare the vegetables and chop the peanuts.

3) Heat vegetable oil in a large wok over medium-high heat, add garlic and chicken, and stir-fry until chicken turns white. Push chicken up the sides of the wok, then pour beaten eggs into the oil on the bottom of the wok. Let eggs cook for a minute before flipping and chopping them up a bit, and then stir eggs in with chicken. A mother and child reunion.

4) Lower the wok heat to medium, add soaked (and well-drained) rice noodles, ketchup, vinegar, sugar, chili flakes, lime juice, ¾ of the bean sprouts, the sliced pepper, half of the green onions, and half of the chopped peanuts. Toss everything together for a few minutes, until it's all mixed up and steaming hot.

To Serve:

Arrange orange slices around the edges of a large platter, pour the Pad Thai into the center, sprinkle with the rest of the peanuts and green onion, and place the remaining sprouts at either end. Drop the lime wedges onto the sprouts. Truly a thing of beauty.

never made it at home? Why? Don't ask me about

SWIMMING TO CAMBODIA: In this film, monologist Spalding Gray sits behind a desk and talks for an hour and a half about his experiences in Thailand while acting in a supporting role on The Killing Fields. He is a compelling and often hilarious storyteller – his anecdotes running the gamut from sex shows in Southeast Asia to life in New York. Completely mesmerizing. Dir: Jonathan Demme. C: Spalding Gray. 1988; 87 m.

FORBIDDEN PLANET: Before 2001 came along, this was *the* space movie. It's a futurized version of Shakespeare's Tempest, in which a mission from Earth crash lands on the planet Altair-4 in the year 2200. Survivors left on Altair-4 include a doctor, his daughter, and Robby the Robot. Then stuff happens. Dir: Fred M. Wilcox. C: Walter Pidgeon, Anne Francis, Leslie Nielsen, Jack Kelly. 1956; 98 m.

THE BRIDGE OVER THE RIVER KWAI: This film, based on Pierre Boulle's novel, is a big-time drama about the futility of war, focusing on a group of British POWs in a Japanese labor camp who are forced to build a bridge that will carry the enemy into the Burmese jungle. I walked across this famous bridge in Thailand. It's kind of rickety and scary. The film swept the Oscars. Dir: David Lean. C: William Holden, Alec Guiness, Jack Hawkins, Sessue Hayakawa. 1957; 162 m.

Moody Crustaceans: Sweet and Sour Shrimp, page 142
Illicit Fowl: Tandoori Chicken, page 128

SWEDISH MEATBALLS WITH DILLED POTATOES
Serves 4

Ingredients:

1 lb. lean ground beef
1 tsp. salt
½ tsp. pepper
1 bottle Heinz chili sauce
½ jar Welch's grape jelly
4 medium potatoes, peeled and quartered
2 tsp. butter
1 tbsp. fresh, chopped dill, or 1 tsp. dried

**Assemble-it-yourself furniture, leggy supermodels, ABBA, and Bergman films
Now add meatballs to the list!**

se:

Method:

1) Season ground beef with salt and pepper, and form into tight, inch-round balls.

2) In a large pot, pour in chili sauce and grape jelly. Bring to a boil. Add meatballs and lower heat to medium. Cover and let simmer for 20 minutes.

3) Meanwhile, peel and quarter potatoes, and put in a medium saucepan. Cover with water and boil (partially covered) for 20 minutes, or until fork-tender. Drain, mix in butter, dill, and salt and pepper to taste.

To Serve:

Give each person 5 or 6 balls and a serving of the dilled taters. Keep the extra sauce standing by so guests can wipe up the mess with bites of meatballs, potatoes, and chunks of bread.

That's what those nutty Swedes are known for.

ELVIRA MADIGAN: A glorious Swedish romance based on a true story about a married army officer who runs off with a tightrope walker. Set to the soaring tunes of Mozart, it's really quite a dreamy picture. Dir: Bo Widerberg. C: Pia Degermark, Thommy Berggren. 1967; 89 m.

FANNY AND ALEXANDERA: This layered drama is based on Swedish filmmaker Ingmar Bergman's own childhood, and it's one of his best efforts. When a young boy's father dies, his mom remarries a minister, curtailing his picture-perfect childhood. Winner of four Oscars, including best foreign film. Dir: Ingmar Bergman. C: Pernilla Allwin, Bertil Guve, Gunn Wallgren, Allan Edwall, Ewa Froling. 1983; 197 m.

MY LIFE AS A DOG: A funny import set in circa 1950s Sweden. A young boy whose mom becomes ill is shipped off to live with his country kin. While there, puberty sets in and takes its toll, including puppy love via the town tomboy. Dir: Lasse Hallstrom. C: Anton Glanzelius, Tomas von Bromssen, Anki Liden. 1987; 101 m.

Illicit Fowl:
TANDOORI CHICKEN
Serves 6

Ingredients:

(Preheat oven to 400 degrees Fahrenheit if baking)

4 lbs. chicken pieces (breasts, legs, thighs), rinsed and patted dry
8 oz. plain yogurt
1 onion, chopped
3 garlic cloves, chopped
1 tbsp. lemon juice
2 tbsp. curry powder
2 tbsp. paprika
2 tsp. salt
1 tsp. ground ginger
½ tsp. cayenne pepper

DO NOT THAW CHICKEN AT ROOM TEMPERATURE. INSTEAD, THAW IT SLOWLY IN THE FRIDGE OR QUICKER IN THE MICROWAVE ON DEFROST.

This is as much about the philosophy of balance as it is about eating. Bitter/
fire of curry is quenched by the cool of yogurt. Grilled on the BBQ or baked

Method:

1) Make 4 or 5 diagonal slashes in each piece of chicken, then set aside in a large ovenproof dish.

2) Combine yogurt, onion, garlic, lemon juice, curry, paprika, salt, ginger, and cayenne pepper. Puree with a hand blender.

3) Pour yogurt mixture over the chicken, flip the pieces around so that they're completely covered, and marinate for a half hour.

4) If barbecuing, heat coals to medium-hot and grill chicken for about 40 minutes, flipping often and basting with mixture left in pan. If baking, put chicken in preheated 400 degree Fahrenheit oven and follow the same cooking directions as barbecuing.

To Serve:

Put chicken on a serving platter and serve with toasted almond-spiked rice, a crunchy salad, and a wedge of lemon.

weet. Hot/cold. Robert De Niro/Chris Farley. The
n the oven, the moist, marinated meat is Nirvana.

BIRD: A perfect biography about the life of jazz great Charlie Parker. The stark portrayal of the saxophone-playing legend doesn't sidestep the realities of his drug-filled life. The moody soundtrack and tender performances make this a must see for all jazz aficionados, and poultry fans. Dir: Clint Eastwood. C: Forest Whitaker, Diane Venora, Michael Zelniker. 1988; 161 m.

INDIA SONG: The lovelorn wife of an emissary to India becomes depressed and tries to overcome her boredom by partaking in several love affairs. This leads to even more self-loathing and an emotional breakdown. A dark film with a star-making turn by Delphine Seyrig. Put on an Indian smorgasbord complete with chicken, dal, and a yoghurt-cucumber salad to cheer you up. Dir: Marguerite Duras. C: Delphine Seyrig, Mathiew Carriere. 1975; 120 m.

ONE FLEW OVER THE CUCKOO'S NEST: Jack Nicholson plays a convict who elects to go to a psychiatric hospital in lieu of prison, thinking he can beat the system. This turns out to be a horrid miscalculation. The film swept the top Oscars and definitely does justice to Ken Kesey's rebellious novel. Once you go cuckoo for this chicken recipe, you'll fit right in. Dir: Milos Forman. C: Jack Nicholson, Louise Fletcher, Brad Dourif, William Redfield, Danny Devito, Christopher Lloyd. 1975; 129 m.

fire wokking
SZECHWAN ORANGE BEEF
Serves 4

Ingredients:

1 lb. top round steak
2 tbsp. soy sauce
2 tsp. cornstarch
1 tsp. sesame oil
2 tbsp. orange peel (pith, white bitter skin, removed), thinly sliced
pinch of sugar
½ cup orange juice
2 tbsp. vegetable oil
½ tbsp. ginger, peeled and minced
2 cloves garlic, minced
1 cup fresh snow pea pods, stems removed
1 green onion, cut in 5 pieces
1 carrot, peeled and thinly sliced
2 red chili peppers, each seeded and sliced in 4
10 oz. can mandarin orange sections, drained
1 orange, sliced into 4 wedges (for garnish)
1 tbsp. chopped peanuts (for garnish)

Yet another savory Oriental dish to add to your repertoire. Tell people you how easy it is to create.

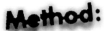

Method:

1) Put the beef in the freezer until partially frozen – about 45 minutes.

2) Slice beef into very thin, bite-sized slices. Set aside. In a small bowl, mix together soy sauce, cornstarch, sesame oil, orange peel, sugar, and orange juice.

3) Heat wok on high, add oil, and stir-fry ginger and garlic for 20 seconds. Add snow pea pods, green onion, carrot, and chili peppers. Stir-fry for 2 minutes, then remove veggies and set aside.

4) Place beef in wok and stir around for several minutes. Drop in a touch more oil if necessary, then add soy sauce mixture. Cook and stir until sauce thickens and bubbles and juices run clear out of beef. Add drained oranges and cooked vegetables and stir around for another several minutes.

To Serve:

Pour the stir-fry out onto a large platter and place two orange wedges at either end. Sprinkle with peanuts. You should probably warn your guests about the spicy chili peppers. Then again, if you don't like your company so much...

ent on the Long March to make this, but we know

SOMETHING WILD: Perhaps not as wild as this succulent beef dish, but this chilling comedy comes pretty damn close. Jeff Daniels is a desk-bound slouch who is picked up by seductress Melanie Griffith, and from there on in, it's one thrilling thing after another. Ray Liotta plays his best character yet; you'll have nightmares about him, guaranteed. Dir: Jonathan Demme. C: Jeff Daniels, Melanie Griffith, Ray Liotta, Margaret Colin, Tracey Walter. 1986; 113 m.

THE MANCHURIAN CANDIDATE: From the Richard Condon novel, it's one part heart-pounding chiller and two parts black comedy. A decorated war veteran, who returns home from Korea, is coaxed into taking out a political rival by his evil mom. A brilliantly acted and directed espionage thriller. Dir: John Frankenheimer. C: Frank Sinatra, Laurence Harvey, Janet Leigh, Angela Lansbury, Henry Silva. 1962; 127 m.

DEAD MAN WALKING: Based on a true story, a nun forges a special relationship with a man who is on death row for the murder of a teenage couple. It's a superb look at capital punishment, the justice system, and the lives that are affected by them. It'll get you thinking. Susan Sarandon won the best actress Oscar for her performance, and Sean Penn was nominated for his. Dir: Tim Robbins. C: Sean Penn, Susan Sarandon. 1995; 122 m.

mysterious flying
MOROCCAN COUSCOUS
Serves 4

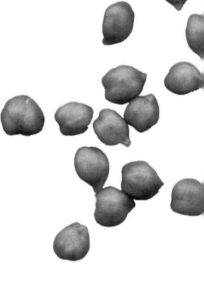

Ingredients:

2 tbsp. butter
½ small red onion, chopped
1 red pepper, chopped
1 small zucchini, chopped
3 tsp. cumin powder
½ tsp. chili flakes
1 ¼ cups chicken or vegetable stock
1 cup instant couscous*
1 can chickpeas, rinsed and drained
½ cup dried apricots, chopped
salt and pepper to taste
¼ cup slivered almonds, toasted
3 tbsp. fresh parsley, chopped

*Couscous is durum wheat semolina, a traditional North African grain that features prominently in Moroccan, Algerian, and Tunisian dishes.

Carpets, markets, smoke, and snake charmers. Welcome to the land of cousco steaming pot of solid nutrition.

vegetab es:

Method:

1) In a medium-sized saucepan over medium heat, melt butter. Add chopped onion, red pepper, and zucchini, and cook for 5 minutes, or until veggies go soft.

2) Add cumin, chili flakes, and chicken (or vegetable) stock. Bring to a boil, add couscous, stir, and add chickpeas and chopped apricots. Cover and remove from heat. Let stand for 5 minutes, then lift off lid, stir, add salt and pepper, and stir in almonds and parsley.

To Serve:

Spoon this colorful dish onto big plates and serve with sliced oranges and red onion, seasoned with parsley, oil, vinegar, and a couple shakes of salt and pepper.

us. With its veggies, nuts, and fruit, couscous is a

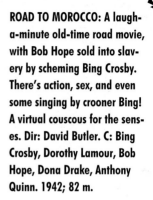

ROAD TO MOROCCO: A laugh-a-minute old-time road movie, with Bob Hope sold into slavery by scheming Bing Crosby. There's action, sex, and even some singing by crooner Bing! A virtual couscous for the senses. Dir: David Butler. C: Bing Crosby, Dorothy Lamour, Bob Hope, Dona Drake, Anthony Quinn. 1942; 82 m.

BAGDAD CAFE: A sprightly West German comedy about a woman who goes through a personal awakening when she leaves her husband in the middle of the Mojave Desert and joins the group of esoteric characters at a roadside cafe. Dir: Percy Adlon. C: Marianne Sagebrecht, CCH Pounder, Jack Palance, Christine Kaufmann. 1988; 91 m.

MEAN STREETS: Director Martin Scorsese breaks all the rules with his primitive camera work, raw energy, pop music, and edgy performances by Robert De Niro and Harvey Keitel. The story is about a racketeer with a heavy conscience, who's trying to keep his trash-talking protégé from getting whacked. If you think Morocco and Bagdad sound dangerous, try New York City on for size. Dir: Martin Scorsese, C: Robert De Niro, Harvey Keitel, David Proval, Amy Robinson, Richard Romanus. 1973; 112 m.

salmon-chante

DIJON SALMON FILLETS
Serves 4

Ingredients:

(Preheat over to 425 degrees Fahrenheit)

4 salmon fillets, about 6 oz. each
¼ cup fresh lemon juice (1 or 2 lemons) + 1 lemon cut into
4 wedges for garnish
1 bunch spinach leaves, well washed
1 bunch fresh dill, ¾ chopped, ¼ not chopped (reserved
for garnish)
¼ cup mayonnaise
1 tbsp. Dijon mustard
½ tsp. Worcestershire sauce
½ tsp. salt
½ tsp. pepper
1 egg white, whipped

**Something's fishy if your stranger in the night doesn't love this fancy dish. I
goodness. Sorry, Charlie.**

d evening:

Method:

1) Marinate salmon fillets in lemon juice for a half hour in the fridge.

2) In a saucepan over medium heat, cook spinach until it's soft, drain well, squeeze out excess water with your hands, then set aside.

3) When the half hour of marinating is almost up, mix together the chopped dill, mayonnaise, Dijon, Worcestershire, salt, and pepper, then carefully fold in the stiff egg white.

4) Remove salmon fillets from the lemon juice and lay them on a baking sheet. Place some cooked spinach over the salmon, then evenly spread the mustard mixture over each spinach-covered fillet. Bake in the preheated 425 degree Fahrenheit oven for 18 to 20 minutes. The topping will rise and brown.

To Serve:

Each person gets a comely salmon fillet, garnished on the side with a bunch of dill and a wedge of lemon. Folks, this is as elegant as it gets.

's moist and marinated and packed with ocean

THE LITTLE MERMAID: When I took my little cousins to see this heartwarming, animated musical, I kept thinking, damn, those crustaceans look good enough to eat. But in truth, I loved the movie, the Oscar-winning soundtrack rocked, and the kids went crazy for the lovable Disney characters. Dir: John Musker, Ron Clements. C: Voices of Jodi Benson, Pat Carroll, Buddy Hackett. 1989; 83 m.

A FISH CALLED WANDA: A wacky caper with a stellar ensemble cast. The plot to double-cross some partners in a jewelry heist takes a ton of hilarious black turns, with something to offend everyone – from lawyers to animal lovers. Dir: Charles Crichton. C: John Cleese, Jamie Lee Curtis, Kevin Kline, Michael Palin. 1988; 108 m.

ON THE WATERFRONT: A rough-edged look at fishy union dealings on the New York waterfront. This classic American tale swept the Oscars, including prizes for best picture, director, actor, supporting actress, screenplay, cinematography, editing, and art direction. Dir: Elia Kazan. C: Marlon Brando, Eva Marie Saint, Karl Malden, Lee J. Cobb, Rod Steiger. 1954; 108 m.

so hot it's co

THE BEST CHILI YOU'LL EVER EAT

Serves 4

Ingredients:

2 tbsp. vegetable oil
1 large onion, chopped
2 cloves garlic, minced
2 celery stalks, chopped
2 carrots, peeled and chopped
1 lb. lean ground beef*
28 oz. can tomatoes, chopped (reserve juice)
6 oz. can tomato paste
1 cup water
1 tsp. brown sugar
2 tbsp. chili powder
10 shakes Tabasco sauce
½ tsp. dry mustard
1 tsp. cumin
1 tsp. Worcestershire sauce
1 tsp. salt
½ tsp. black pepper
1 bay leaf
16 oz. can red kidney beans, drained and rinsed

Thick and meaty and full of sexual potential, it's a healthy, easy dish, compl

ol:

*To make this chili suitable for herbivores, substitute the ground beef with one cup of texturized vegetable protein (TVP), available at health food stores. Follow the recipe as usual – except omit the meat – and add the TVP after adding the tomatoes and spices.

Method:

1) In a large pot, heat oil on medium, then add chopped onion, garlic, celery, and carrots, and cook for several minutes. Add the ground meat and cook for 5 minutes, breaking it up with a wooden spoon. Do the hokey-pokey and stir it all around.

2) Add remaining ingredients except the beans, then bring the mixture to a boil. Lower heat to medium-low and let simmer, partially covered, for a half hour. Stir every so often. Add the drained can of beans and cook for at least another half hour, or until most of the liquid has evaporated and your chili looks like chili (as opposed to chili soup).

To Serve:

Call me crazy, but I'm thinking a big bowlful of chili would go mighty nice with a hunk of Kick The Can: Mexican Corn Bread (recipe p.32).

te with a snazzy vegetarian option. Wicked cool.

BLAZING SADDLES: This film includes the funniest moment ever recorded on celluloid. I'll give you a hint – beans and noxious gases are involved. A hilarious Western spoof in which a black man is appointed sheriff of an all-white town. Chili and cornbread and farts all around! Dir: Mel Brooks. C: Cleavon Little, Gene Wilder, Harvey Korman, Madeline Kahn. 1974; 93 m.

GAS.S.S.S.: An innovative comedy in which an experimental gas is released from an Alaskan defense plant, causing everyone on the planet over 30 to croak. An oddball sci-fi flick with loads of laughs. Dir: Roger Corman. C: Bud Cort, Cindy Williams, Ben Vereen, Talia Shire. 1970; 90 m.

HEARTBURN: Don't worry, the chili won't really give you heartburn (if you have Peptol Bismol on hand). The story centers around the breakup of a marriage between a food writer and a political columnist, based on writer Nora Ephron's life and best-selling book. Dir: Mike Nichols. C: Meryl Streep, Jack Nicholson, Jeff Daniels, Maureen Stapleton. 1986; 109 m.

HONEY-GARLIC CHICKEN PIECES

Serves 4

Ingredients:

(Preheat oven to 350 degrees Fahrenheit)

6 assorted chicken pieces, like breasts and legs, rinsed under cool water and patted dry
¾ cup brown sugar
2 tsp. dry mustard powder
4 cloves garlic, minced
3 tbsp. soy sauce
1 ½ cups honey

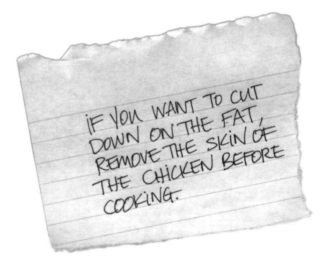

IF YOU WANT TO CUT DOWN ON THE FAT, REMOVE THE SKIN OF THE CHICKEN BEFORE COOKING.

Satisfy your oral fixation with some honey, chicken, and a recipe the Colonel lick your fingers.

Method:

1) Place cleaned chicken pieces in a roasting pan or Pyrex dish. Choose a pan that's just big enough so that the chicken fits in snugly.

2) Evenly distribute the ingredients in the order they appear on the list of ingredients, topping it all off with a shiny coat of honey.

3) Place the dish in the middle rack of the preheated 350 degree Fahrenheit oven, uncovered, and bake for 40 to 50 minutes. Flip pieces over halfway through baking.

4) Using a large spoon or a baster, baste the chicken every 10 minutes with the juices in the pan. Turn pieces over so that they are right side up for the final 10 minutes of baking.

5) To check for doneness, cut a slit into a piece of chicken in the middle of the dish. If the juices run clean, push up those sleeves and get out the wet naps!

To Serve:

Give each person 1 piece of chicken to start. Serve with a side of noodles, or rice, and a vegetable stir-fry. Finger-lickin' good.

never imagined. Finally, a legitimate reason to

THE BIRDS: Once you've seen this horror-filled Alfred Hitchcock classic, you'll likely never feed pigeons again. Top-notch special effects make the series of bird attacks almost too real, as a million feathered varmints descend upon small town U.S.A. Get your revenge; eat sticky chicken! Dir: Alfred Hitchcock. C: Rod Taylor, Tippi Hedren, Suzanne Plechette, Jessica Tandy. 1963; 119 m.

BIRDY: A harrowing tale of two Vietnam veterans who form an unlikely friendship after the war. Birdy (Matthew Modine), who was unstable before his tour of duty, now finds himself slipping in and out of reality and wanting to fly away from his problems. Friend Nicolas Cage gives a stellar performance trying to keep his pal "stuck" to earth. Dir: Alan Parker. C: Matthew Modine, Nicolas Cage, John Harkins, Sandy Baron, Karen Young, Bruno Kirby. 1985; 120 m.

TO KILL A MOCKINGBIRD: You've read the Harper Lee book, now catch the flick. The Depression was bad enough, but add the racist South to the mix, and you've got a sticky situation. Oscar winner Gregory Peck plays a reserved lawyer defending an innocent black man who stands accused of rape. The trial is riveting. Dir: Robert Mulligan. C: Gregory Peck, Mary Badham, Philip Alford, Brock Peters, Robert Duvall. 1962; 129 m.

THREE-MUSHROOM RISOTTO
Serves 4

Ingredients:

THIS IS A DISH YOUR GUESTS CAN HELP WITH. WHILE YOU PREPARE THE REST OF THE FOOD, THEY CAN STIR FOR YOU.

3 oz. packet sliced, dried porcini mushrooms
(available at specialty food shops)
4 cups chicken stock
2 tbsp. unsalted butter
2 cloves garlic, minced
1 small onion, chopped
1 ½ cups Arborio rice*
2 cups fresh button mushrooms, wiped clean and chopped
1 small portobello mushroom, sliced
1 tbsp. Madeira wine (optional)
½ cup grated Parmesan cheese
¼ cup chopped parsley

*Arborio is a short, fat variety of rice and the key ingredient to making a successful risotto. You cannot substitute the arborio with any other kind of rice. If you do, it's your funeral.

You'll have to invest some energy in preparing this baby, so suit up into workout gear and turn on the tunes while you stir and stir and stir. It isn't really that hard, I'm just being an alarmist. Besides, it's worth it; live a little.

n-gi:

Method:

1) Rehydrate the dried porcini mushrooms by soaking them in a cup of boiling water for 45 minutes. At the 40-minute mark, bring the chicken stock to a boil in a small pot.

2) In a medium-sized saucepan, melt the butter over low heat, then cook the chopped onion and garlic in the melted butter, until slightly browned. Add the arborio rice and stir well.

3) Make sure the chicken stock is simmering on the stove, so there's easy access to it as you slowly add it to the pot of buttered rice. Stir 1 cup of stock into the rice, bring to a boil (stir often so it doesn't stick), and allow almost all of the liquid to evaporate before adding another cup of stock. After the second cup of stock has been absorbed, add the chopped porcini mushrooms (with the liquid they were soaking in) and the button and portobello mushrooms. Keep stirring. Add another cup of stock, let it evaporate (keep stirring), and add the remaining stock. Stir baby, stir.

4) From start to finish, it should take between 20 and 30 minutes to prepare the risotto. Then turn the heat down to low, add the Madeira wine, Parmesan cheese, and all but a ½ tbsp. of the chopped parsley. Stir well.

5) Cover and let cook for 3 minutes. Then go ice that elbow.

To Serve:

Dish it up while it's hot, and sprinkle each plate with parsley. Then, if you're feeling cheeky, walk around the table with a mammoth pepper mill and ask your guests if they would like fresh pepper, just like in a restaurant. And keep the wine flowing.

BIG NIGHT: Two Italian immigrant brothers want to be true to their culinary art when they open up their own restaurant in 1950s, spaghetti and meatballs America. The only problem is, they're going broke while trying to explain to their patrons that risotto is a main dish, not to be served with a side of spag. Pop this low-budget charmer in the VCR and try to duplicate the gorgeous dinner party at the film's climax. Include antipasto, pizzas, risotto, the ricotta dessert, and fresh fruit. Dir: Stanley Tucci, Campbell Scott. C: Tony Shalhoub, Stanley Tucci, Minnie Driver. 1996; 107 m.

CINEMA PARADISO: A 5-hanky sobber set in post-WW II Italy. A sprightly young boy in love with the movies hitches himself to the local projectionist, whereupon they form a lifelong friendship. This moving homage to the cinema won the Oscar for best foreign film. Dir: Giuseppe Tornatore. C: Philippe Noiret, Jacques Perrin, Salvatore Cascio. 1989; 123 m.

BITTER RICE: This Italian neorealist beauty is about female rice pickers who work hard by day and even harder by night (if you know what I mean — wink, wink). Might just put you in the mood for some sexy risotto. Dir: Giuseppe De Santis. C: Silvana Mangano, Vittorio Gassman, Raf Vallone. 1948; 107 m.

moody crust

SWEET AND SOUR SHRIMP
Serves 4

Ingredients:

1 tbsp. vegetable oil
2 garlic cloves, minced
1 onion, chopped
1 tsp. fresh ginger, peeled and finely chopped
1 green pepper, cored and chopped
1 red pepper, cored and chopped
2 carrots, peeled and thinly sliced
2 stalks celery, sliced
2 tsp. cornstarch mixed with 1 tbsp. water
1 lb. fresh shrimp, peeled and deveined*
19 oz. can pineapple chunks, drained, but juice reserved
½ cup ketchup
1 tbsp. brown sugar
2 tbsp. soy sauce
1 lemon, juiced
5 shakes Tabasco sauce

It used to be that when we ordered in Chinese food, they always dropped th
Whether we ordered 4 dishes or 8, how did they know there were 6 of us? A

aceans:

*The fishmonger can prepare the shrimp for you, or you can do it yourself by cutting a little slit down their backs, peeling off the shells, and picking out the black thread (that's the poop). If you don't fancy seafood, substitute shrimp with 4 boneless, skinless chicken breasts or a pound of firm, cubed tofu. If using chicken or tofu, cook first in oil for 5 minutes, remove, set aside, and follow recipe from step #1.

Method:

1) Heat oil in wok on medium-high heat. Stir-fry the garlic, onion, ginger, green and red peppers, carrots, and celery. Keep tossing around for about 5 minutes.

2) In a small bowl or cup, mix cornstarch with water.

3) Stir in prepared shrimp, then add half the pineapple juice (drink the rest!), ketchup, brown sugar, cornstarch mixture, soy sauce, lemon, and Tabasco. Let cook for several minutes, stir in pineapple, and cook for another minute.

To Serve:

Simply succulent over a bed of steamed rice.

e right number of fortune cookies in the bag.
n age-old mystery.

SWEET AND SOUR: A comical homage to the French New Wave cinema. A group of French cinephiles tip their berets to their filmmaking heroes. A little bit sweet and a little bit sour, it's not for everyone but definitely for movie connoisseurs. Dir: Jacques Baratier. C: Guy Bedos, Jean-Pierre Marielle, Sophie Daumier. 1964; 93 m.

FORREST GUMP: Through the magic of special effects, simpleton Tom Hanks has quite the life — from meeting several presidents, to running across America. He also becomes a multimillionaire along the way. Not bad for a supposedly retarded man. And how did he amass his fortune? Shrimp, my boy. Dir: Robert Zemeckis. C: Tom Hanks, Robin Wright, Sally Field, Gary Sinise, Mykelti Williamson. 1994; 90 m.

DOUBLE HAPPINESS: A Chinese-Canadian woman is torn between the values and traditions of her Old World parents and the freewheeling spirit of her Canadian self. It's a quirky comedy with a plethora of charming performances. Dir: Mina Shum. C: Sandra Oh, Allanah Ong, Stephen Chang, Johnny Mah. 1995; 87 m.

courtesy of John Katsuras

pizzas and pastas

pizza perfect and sea
DOUGHS, SAUCES, AND TOPPINGS

Whole-Wheat Herb Pizza Dough
(Makes four 12-inch pizzas)

Ingredients:

1 package dry yeast
2 cups warm water
2 eggs
2 tbsp. sugar
4 tbsp. olive oil
1 tsp. salt
3 cups whole-wheat flour
2 cups all-purpose flour
½ tsp. dried oregano
¼ tsp. chili flakes
½ tsp. dried basil

Method:

1) Stir yeast into water and let sit for 10 minutes.

2) In a large bowl, whisk the yeast mixture with the eggs, sugar, oil, and salt, until foamy.

3) Slowly mix in the 5 cups of flour and

IF YOU WANT A STRAIGHT-AHEAD, PLAIN DOUGH, REPLACE WHOLE-WHEAT FLOUR WITH ALL-PURPOSE AND CUT OUT THE HERBS.

the herbs, mixing well until the wet ingredients are absorbed. Once all of the flour has been added, the dough should be soft but not sticky. Add more flour if necessary.

4) Divide dough into 5 even rounds. Brush with a bit of oil, cover with a tea towel, and let it rise for about an hour in a warm place. When dough has doubled in size, punch it down.

To Serve:

Spin dough out a bit, then place on a sprayed pizza pan. Pat it down with your fingertips. Once your toppings of choice have been added, bake in a pre-

heated 400 degree Fahrenheit oven for about 20 minutes, or until the crust has browned, and the top is bubbly. Unused portions of dough can be wrapped and stored in the freezer.

Instant Pizza Dough
(Makes one 12-inch pizza)

Ingredients:

½ tsp. sugar
½ tsp. salt
1 cup flour
¼ cup Crisco vegetable shortening
1 tbsp. olive oil
1 ½ tbsp. milk
1 egg, beaten

Method:

1) In a medium-sized bowl, mix the sugar, salt, and flour together. Then add the vegetable shortening and mix into the flour using your hands. It

Generation X? I don't think so. Our friend Doug Coupland would have sold Which is where I come in. Here are the secret recipes for the best in sauces, change a life, they taste great.

146

utively saucy:

should resemble fine breadcrumbs after a while.

2) Add oil, milk, and egg, and work it all together until it forms a ball of dough.

3) Sprinkle a bit of flour over a flat surface and knead the dough for 2 minutes, until soft and smooth.

To Serve:

Press the dough into a 12-inch sprayed pizza pan, brush with oil, add your toppings, and bake in a preheated 400 degree Fahrenheit oven for about 20 minutes.

To MAKE A DEEP-DISH PIZZA, SPRAY AN 8-INCH PIE PAN WITH VEGETABLE OIL AND PRESS THE DOUGH INTO THE PAN AND UP THE SIDES. THEN FILL WITH YOUR FAVORITE TOPPINGS AND BAKE FOR AN ADDITIONAL 10 MINUTES.

any more books if he'd called us Generation Pizza.
oughs, and pizzas. They define a lifestyle, they

MYSTIC PIZZA: A slice-of-life drama involving three women who work at a pizza parlor in the resort town of Mystic, Connecticut. The trio of newcomer actresses are hot without being too cheesy, but it's the pizza that steals the show. What is the secret ingredient? Dir: Donald Petrie. C: Annabeth Gish, Julia Roberts, Lili Taylor. 1988; 102 m.

THE PIZZA TRIANGLE: Amore, Italian style. Two equally engaging men compete for the heart of the same woman. Lovely photography and superb acting makes this satire more than just silly. Dir: Ettore Scola. C: Marcello Mastroianni, Monica Vitti, Giancarlo Giannini. 1970; 99 m.

Roasted Eggplant, Red Pepper, and Artichoke Pizza, page 152

Cheeseburger Pizza

(Makes one 12-inch pizza)

Preheat oven to 400 degrees Fahrenheit

Ingredients:

1 tbsp. olive oil
½ lb. lean ground beef
1 garlic clove, minced
1 small onion, chopped
¼ tsp. salt
2 tbsp. mayonnaise
2 tsp. ketchup
2 tsp. relish
1 ball prepared Instant Pizza Dough
(or 12-inch store-bought pizza shell)
1 large dill pickle, sliced
1 cup cheddar cheese, shredded
2 cups iceberg lettuce, shredded
2 tomatoes, cored and chopped

Method:

1) In a small frying pan, heat oil over medium heat, add ground beef, garlic, onion, and salt, and cook for 7 minutes or until juices run clear. Drain off any liquid and set aside.

2) In a small bowl, mix together mayo with ketchup and relish. This is the "special sauce."
3) Press pizza dough out onto a pizza pan or place a bought shell on the pan. Spread with "special sauce," sliced pickle, and ground beef. Then top with an even layer of cheese and bake in the preheated 400 degree Fahrenheit oven for about 20 minutes or until dough is baked and cheese is melted and slightly browned.

To Serve:

Call everyone to the table, take the hot pie out of the oven, top with shredded lettuce and chopped tomatoes, slice, and serve immediately. Then sit down and grab yourself a slice or 2 because you deserve a break today.

Chévre and Salmon Pizza

(Makes one 12-inch pizza)

Preheat oven to 400 degrees Fahrenheit

Ingredients:

1 tbsp. olive oil
¼ tsp. chili flakes
1 tbsp. fresh dill, chopped
6 oz. chèvre
1 ball prepared Whole-Wheat Herb Pizza Dough (or a 12-inch store-bought pizza shell)
6 oz. skinless salmon fillet, cut into ½-inch slices
salt and pepper to taste

Method:

1) In a small bowl, mix olive oil with chili flakes. Set aside.

2) In another small bowl, mix chopped dill in with chèvre.

3) Press prepared dough into a pizza pan or place store-bought shell on pan and spread with chèvre. Toss salmon slices with olive oil mixture, then layer

uctively saucy

slices over chèvre-topped pizza. Sprinkle with salt and pepper.

4) Bake in the preheated 400 degree Fahrenheit oven for about 20 minutes or until dough is brown around the edges and salmon is cooked through.

To Serve:

Drizzle the pizza with a little additional olive oil before slicing and serving. An extra sprinkling of dill would also be a nice touch.

Pineapple Pizza

(Makes one 12-inch pizza)

Preheat oven to 400 degrees Fahrenheit

Ingredients:

1 ball prepared Instant Pizza Dough (or 12-inch store-bought pizza shell)
4 tbsp. Basic Tomato Sauce (or store-bought tomato sauce)
2 cups mozzarella cheese, shredded
¼ tsp. chili flakes
1 tsp. dried oregano
½ tsp. dried basil
½ cup red onion, chopped
6 green olives, sliced
½ cup pineapple chunks

Method:

1) Press prepared dough into a pizza pan or place store-bought shell on pan and spread with tomato sauce.

2) Top with shredded cheese, chili flakes, oregano, and basil. Then sprinkle evenly with prepared vegetables and drained pineapple chunks.

3) Bake in the preheated 400 degree Fahrenheit oven for about 20 minutes or until dough is brown around the edges and vegetables are cooked.

To Serve:

Hack it up and dish it out.

Roasted Eggplant, Red Pepper, and Artichoke Pizza

(Makes one 12-inch pizza)

Preheat oven to 400 degrees Fahrenheit

Ingredients:

½ small eggplant, sliced into thin rounds
2 tbsp. olive oil
2 tsp. soy sauce
1 ball prepared Whole-Wheat Herb Pizza Dough (or store-bought 12-inch pizza shell)
3 tbsp. Basic Tomato Sauce (or store-bought tomato sauce)
1 cup mozzarella cheese, grated
½ cup bottled roasted red peppers, drained and chopped
1 jar artichoke hearts, drained and chopped
½ cup Parmesan cheese, grated
½ tsp. dried oregano
½ tsp. dried basil
¼ tsp. chili flakes

Method:

1) Wash and slice eggplant into thin rounds, then brush each side with a mixture of olive oil and soy sauce. Place on a cookie sheet and broil on both sides until browned. Set aside.

2) Press fresh dough out onto a pizza pan (or place prepared crust on pan) and spread evenly with tomato sauce. Sprinkle with shredded mozzarella, then arrange prepared vegetables in an even and artistic fashion. Top with parmesan and seasonings, then bake in preheated 400 degree Fahrenheit oven for about 20 minutes, or until crust is browned and pizza looks bubbly hot – and good enough to eat.

To Serve:

This ain't rocket science. Slice it up and people will grab and eat.

DON'T THROW OUT THE FLAVORFUL OIL LEFT BEHIND IN THE ARTICHOKE JAR. IT IS PERFECT FOR MARINATING CHICKEN OR FISH AND ALSO MAKES A GREAT SALAD DRESSING. WASTE NOT, WANT NOT.

Sausage and Apple Pizza

(Makes one 12-inch pizza)

Preheat oven to 400 degrees Fahrenheit

Ingredients:

2 links Italian sausage
2 McIntosh apples, each cored, peeled, and sliced into 8 wedges
¼ tsp. cinnamon
1 tbsp. maple syrup
1 ball prepared Whole-Wheat Herb Pizza Dough (or 12-inch store-bought pizza shell)
2 cups cheddar cheese, shredded

Method:

1) In a small pot, bring water to a boil. Poke sausages several times with a fork, then boil for 5 minutes. Drain and slice into 1-inch slices.

2) Take prepared apples and toss with cinnamon and maple syrup.

3) Press prepared dough into a pizza pan or place store-bought shell on pan and sprinkle with shredded cheese. Top

uctively saucy

with apple slices and sausage, and bake in the preheated 400 degree Fahrenheit oven for about 20 minutes or until dough is brown around the edges, apples are soft, and cheese is melted.

To Serve:

Let the pizza sit for a minute before slicing and serving.

Wild Mushroom and Pesto Pizza
(Makes one 12-inch pizza)

Preheat oven to 400 degrees Fahrenheit

Ingredients:

3 oz. packet dried, sliced porcini mushrooms
1 tsp. butter
1 tsp. olive oil
1 portobello mushroom, sliced
5 button mushrooms, sliced
salt and pepper to taste
1 ball prepared Whole-Wheat Herb Pizza Dough (or a 12-inch store-bought pizza shell)

2 tbsp. Pesto Sauce With Sundried Tomatoes (or store-bought pesto)
2 cups mozzarella cheese, shredded

Method:

1) Boil a cup of water and rehydrate porcini mushrooms in the hot water for 45 minutes. After the time's up, drain, chop, and set aside.

2) Heat butter and oil in a medium-sized frying pan, add sliced portobello and button mushrooms, and sauté for 5 minutes. Add salt and pepper to taste.

3) Press prepared dough into a pizza pan or place store-bought shell on pan and spread with pesto. Then sprinkle with all the mushrooms and top with cheese.

4) Bake in the preheated 400 degree Fahrenheit oven for about 20 minutes or until dough is brown around the edges and mozzarella is melted.

To Serve:

Slice into even wedges, then sit back and take in the praise. Make this one of several pizzas you offer at a party.

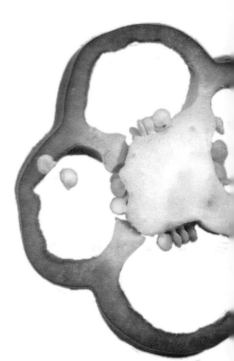

Each recipe makes about
2 cups of sauce

Basic Tomato Sauce

Ingredients:

2 tbsp. olive oil
4 garlic cloves, minced
2 28 oz. cans plum tomatoes, drained
and chopped
½ cup dry red wine
2 tsp. dried basil
1 tsp. dried oregano
1 bay leaf
½ tsp. sugar
½ tsp. salt
¼ tsp. black pepper

Method:

In a medium-sized pot over medium-low heat, add the oil and garlic, and cook for 2 minutes, making sure the garlic doesn't burn. Add remaining ingredients and simmer over medium-low heat for an hour, stirring every so often. Taste and adjust seasonings to taste.

Spicy Arrabiatta Sauce

Follow the same directions as Basic Tomato Sauce, but add 2 additional garlic cloves and one tsp. of chili pepper flakes to the list of ingredients.

Chunky Vegetable Sauce

Follow the same directions as Basic Tomato Sauce, but when cooking the garlic in the olive oil, add ½ cup sliced mushrooms, ¼ cup chopped green pepper, ¼ cup chopped onion, and 5 sliced green olives. Cook for an additional 2 minutes before adding remaining ingredients.

Meat Sauce

Follow the same directions as Basic Tomato Sauce, but when cooking the garlic, add ¼ lb. lean ground beef and cook for 4 minutes, breaking up the meat with a wooden spoon.

Pesto Sauce With Sundried Tomatoes
(Makes 1 cup)

Ingredients:

25 fresh basil leaves
2 tbsp. fresh parsley, chopped
5 garlic cloves
⅓ cup Parmesan cheese
⅓ cup pine nuts, toasted
½ tsp. salt
4 sundried tomatoes, rehydrated and
drained*
1 tbsp. lemon juice
½ cup olive oil

*Sundried tomatoes can be found in specialty food shops, and the produce or bulk food section of the supermarket. To rehydrate them, simmer in a small pot of boiling water for 5 minutes.

Method:

Using a hand blender, mix the basil together with parsley, garlic, Parmesan, pine nuts, salt, tomatoes, and lemon juice. When well blended, gradually add in the olive oil until it becomes a smooth sauce.

nd friends

Alfredo Sauce

Ingredients:

1 cup whipping cream
2 cloves garlic, minced
2 tbsp. butter
½ tsp. salt
¼ tsp. black pepper
⅔ cup grated Parmesan cheese

Method:

In a medium saucepan over medium-low heat, pour in ⅔ cup of cream, stir in the garlic, butter, salt, and pepper. Simmer for 5 minutes, allowing the sauce to thicken. Make sure it never boils. Add remaining cream, cook for 3 more minutes, then add the cheese and cook for a few more minutes, or until sauce is thick. Taste and adjust seasoning.

Pasta Pairings And Toppings

The following pairings are merely suggestions. Anything goes. As for serving size, 1 lb. of pasta serves approximately 4 people. When it comes time to dish out the pasta, you'll want to stir in just enough sauce to coat the pasta.

Basic Tomato Sauce goes well with spaghetti, capellini, penne, and farfalle.
Spicy Arrabiatta Sauce goes well with penne, farfalle, and orecchiette.
Chunky Vegetable Sauce goes well with spaghetti, linguine, and radiatore.
Meat Sauce goes well with rigatoni, spaghetti, and fusilli.
Pesto Sauce With Sundried Tomatoes goes well with fusilli, penne, and capellini.
Alfredo Sauce goes well with fettuccine and linguine.

Pasta Toppings

Like pizza, pasta is a blank canvas, out of which you can create your own idea of the perfect dish. Once you've paired up your pasta with a choice of sauce, here are some delicious toppings to add to the mix: roasted red peppers, sautéed sliced mushrooms, chopped olives, fresh chopped basil, crumbled chèvre, shaved Parmesan, chopped artichoke hearts, sliced smoked salmon, sliced Italian sausage.

DAYS OF WINE AND ROSES: Don't let the title fool you; this isn't about parties and love. Rather, it's a searing drama about a disintegrating marriage between an alcoholic husband and the wife he brings along for the ride. The title song was an Oscar winner. Dir: Blake Edwards. C: Jack Lemmon, Lee Remick, Charles Bickford, Jack Klugman. 1962; 138 m.

LADY AND THE TRAMP: An animated sweetheart in which highbred cocker spaniel (Lady) and garrulous mongrel (the Tramp) experience the city together and, in a particularly touching scene, share a bowl of spaghetti and meatballs. The kids will love the characters and great songs. Dir: Hamilton Luske, Clyde Geronimi, Wilfred Jackson. 1955; 75 m.

YOU ARE ALWAYS IN A CONSTANT STATE OF DESIRE

courtesy of Melanie Barter

desserts

9½ positions

CHOCOLATE-DIPPED STRAWBERRIES
Makes 1 pint of berries

Ingredients:

1 pint strawberries, washed and dried
5 oz. semisweet chocolate (I use Baker's)
1 ½ tbsp. table cream (18%)

The luscious, juicy berries coupled with the dark, mournful chocolate make t from a stiletto shoe is the beverage of choice.

Method:

1) Set washed strawberries out on the counter until they come to room temperature.

2) Gently melt the chocolate over low heat, then stir in the cream.

3) Working quickly, grab each strawberry by the stem and dip in hot chocolate, halfway up each berry. Place dipped berries on a sheet of tinfoil and put in the fridge to cool.

To Serve:

Open the refrigerator all the way. Blindfold your partner and start pouring honey and milk and all sorts of crap all over their body. Then lick it all off. If you're still hungry after that, pop a few chocolate-covered strawberries in your mouth.

e perfect après the sack, snack. Champagne sipped

LIKE WATER FOR CHOCOLATE: A deliciously sexy Mexican treat about a woman who throws herself, literally, into her cooking. From broiled peppers, that made an entire wedding party horny, to a fowl dish, that made her evil sister ill, our heroine has the secret recipe for making this film supremely luscious. Adapted from the book by Laura Esquivel. Dir: Alfonso Arau. C: Lumi Cavazos, Marco Leonardi. 1992; 113 m.

STRAWBERRY AND CHOCO-LATE: A Cuban delicacy about the improbable friendship that is forged between a gay intellectual and a straight communist. This seemingly light comedy with dramatic undertones is both bitter and sweet. Dir: Tomas Gutierrez Alea, Juan Carlos Tabio. C: Jorge Perrugoria, Vladimir Cruz. 1993; 110 m.

WILD STRAWBERRIES: An Ingmar Bergman classic in which an aging professor reviews his life's disappointments (with effective use of flashbacks), in this marvelously photographed, soaring drama. Quite an emotional experience, especially for retiring profs. Dir: Ingmar Bergman. C: Victor Sjostrom, Ingrid Thulin, Bibi Anderson. 1957; 90 m.

They're Like Buttah: Toblerone Chunk Shortbread Cookies, page 176

fresh and fo

APPLE CRISP WITH FRUIT SALAD
Serves 8

Ingredients:

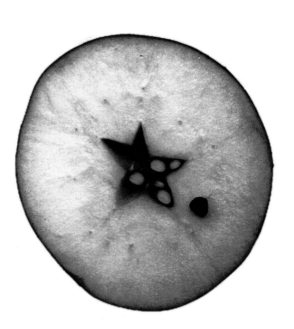

(Preheat oven to 350 degrees Fahrenheit)

4 cups apples (about 6 apples), each peeled and
cored and sliced into 8 wedges
1 tbsp. lemon juice
3 tbsp. sugar (plus 1 tsp. sugar for fruit salad)
vegetable oil spray
⅓ cup brown sugar
½ cup rolled oats
¼ cup chopped pecans
3 tbsp. flour
2 tsp. cinnamon
2 tbsp. butter, melted
4 cups fresh, chopped mixed fruit (strawberries, apples, pears,
oranges, kiwi, grapes, bananas, blueberries, for example)
1 tbsp. chopped mint
½ cup orange juice

Apples, peaches, pears, and plums, tell me when your birthday comes. Janua I'll tell you, those schoolhood days were heady times. Worth reliving in this

ncy:

Method:

1) Combine sliced apples with lemon juice and 3 tbsp. of white sugar, then pour into a 7 x 11-inch Pyrex dish sprayed with vegetable oil. In a small bowl, mix together brown sugar, rolled oats, pecans, flour, and cinnamon. Add melted butter, mix together, and sprinkle over apple mixture. Put in preheated 350 degree Fahrenheit oven and bake for about 50 minutes.

2) Mix prepared chopped fruit in a bowl with 1 tbsp. sugar, mint, and orange juice.

To Serve:

Let the baked apple crisp cool for several minutes before serving. Scoop into funky dessert dishes and side it up with the colorful fruit salad and a cup of joe.

ry, February, March, April, May...Remember that?
ealthy dessert concoction.

APPLESEED: A sexy, Japanese, animated sci-fi thriller set in the post WW III city of Olympus. Two elite cops do battle with evil terrorists armed with lethal "power-suits." May be a little too scary for the kinder, so send them off to bed with a dish of seedless crumble. Dir: Kazuyashi Katayama. 1988; 70 m.

CRUMB: Talk about your dysfunctional families! In this superbly disturbing documentary, '60's underground cartoonist Robert "keep on truckin'" Crumb's life is put under the microscope. His genius and dark humor are often overshadowed by his contempt for American society. I'll bet his mama never made yummy apple desserts. Dir: Terry Zwigoff. C: Robert Crumb, Beatrice Crumb. 1995; 119 m.

SWEET NOTHING: A low-budget tearjerker about a Wall Street star, brought to his knees by the evils of crack cocaine. The wife and kids stand by him as long as possible, but that crack is bad stuff. If only he had just said "yes" to the temptation of this apple dessert instead. Dir: Gary Winick. C: Mira Sorvino, Michael Imperioli, Paul Calderon. 1996; 90 m.

CHOCOLATE PECAN PIE
Serves 8

Ingredients:

(Preheat oven to 350 degrees Fahrenheit)

¼ cup butter (melted) + 2 tbsp. butter (softened)
1 ½ cups chocolate wafers (about 25 cookies), finely ground
vegetable oil spray
½ cup semisweet chocolate chips
1 cup sugar
2 eggs, beaten
1 tsp. vanilla
¼ tsp. salt
¾ cup whole pecans
1 cup whipping cream, whipped

MAKE SURE THE PIE IS COMPLETELY COOLED BEFORE CUTTING. I KNOW IT'S HARD TO WAIT SOMETIMES, BUT IF YOU CUT INTO IT TOO SOON, IT'LL OOZE ALL OVER THE COUNTER, AND WHAT YOU'LL BE LEFT WITH IS NO PIE AND ONE BIG MESS.

Just about every time I go out favorites, but sometimes I get b

Method:

1) To make the crust, mix the melted butter with the cookie crumbs and pat down firmly into a sprayed 9-inch pie pan. Bake for 10 minutes in the preheated 350 degree Fahrenheit oven. Remove and set aside.

2) In a medium-sized bowl, mix together the chocolate chips, softened butter, sugar, beaten eggs, vanilla, and salt. Pour into prepared crust and sprinkle the pecans on top. Bake in preheated 350 degree Fahrenheit oven for 45 minutes. When done (crusty on top) allow it to cool for several hours.

3) Just before serving, whip cream into firm peaks.

To Serve:

Cut the room temperature pie into 8 even slices and plop a dollop of whipped cream beside each piece. I'll be right over.

for dessert I order pecan pie. It's one of my all-time ummed because it's not chocolate. Problem solved.

CHOCOLAT: An evocative look at race relations seen through the eyes of a French woman, as she reminisces about her childhood as the daughter of a French colonist in Africa. We may be different colors on the outside, but we're all the same on the inside. And we all love chocolate! Dir: Claire Denis. C: Isaach DeBankole, Giulia Boschi, Francois Cluzet, Cecile Ducasse. 1989; 105 m.

THE SUGARLAND EXPRESS: A none-too-bright couple on the lam from the law, head out to Sugarland, Texas, to find their boy. During their journey and subsequent search, they become the stars of a media circus. A comedy/drama with Goldie Hawn at her best. This is Steven Spielberg's first big feature. Dir: Steven Spielberg. C: Goldie Hawn, Michael Sacks, William Atherton, Ben Johnson. 1974; 109 m.

TOUCH OF EVIL: A touch of this and a bit of that makes for a deliciously evil pie. A touch of mystery and a bit of intrigue makes for an outrageous crime flick. Here, a Mexican drug cop and his American wife become entangled in a murder investigation at a smarmy border town. Director Orson Welles uses some innovative camera work to make this a classic of its genre. Dir: Orson Welles. C: Charlton Heston, Orson Welles, Janet Leigh. 1958; 108 m.

CIGARETTES IS HEALTHY FOR YOUR BODY

Makes about 60 cigarettes

Ingredients:

(Preheat oven to 350 degrees Fahrenheit)

1 package phyllo sheets (about 16 sheets)
8 tbsp. unsalted butter, melted
1 cup shelled pistachios, finely chopped
1 cup sugar
1 tbsp. orange blossom water or almond extract
¼ cup icing sugar

ALWAYS PREHEAT AN OVEN BEFORE USING IT. THIS PREVENTS THE FOOD YOU'RE BAKING FROM BURNING WHILE THE OVEN IS HEATING UP. WITH MOST OVENS, YOU'LL KNOW IT'S READY TO USE WHEN THE LITTLE RED LIGHT BESIDE THE TEMPERATURE DIAL GOES OUT.

Alert all pregnant women, ex-smokers, and any others who want a supreme healthy. Quitting never tasted this good.

pistachio

Method:

1) Cut the package of phyllo sheets into 6 rectangles, approximately 4 ½" x 7".*

2) Lightly brush each sheet with melted butter.

3) Mix chopped pistachios with sugar and orange blossom water to form the filling.

4) Put 1 tsp. of filling at one short end of each rectangle. Fold the long edges over slightly and roll up into a tight cigarette shape.

5) Place on a greased cookie sheet and brush the top of each pastry with butter.

6) Bake at 350 degrees Fahrenheit for 12 to 15 minutes, until cigarettes turn a golden brown.

*Keep phyllo sheets between sheets of wax paper and covered with a damp tea towel.

To Serve:

When cool, sprinkle cigarettes with icing sugar.

y excellent snack. Smoking pistachio pastries is

CHINATOWN: A gritty film noir that sees Jack Nicholson as a private dick, hired by a mysterious woman to tail her husband. A riveting show with an ending that'll have you inhaling pistachio cigarette after pistachio cigarette. Dir: Roman Polanski. C: Jack Nicholson, Faye Dunaway, John Huston. 1974; 131 m.

WILD AT HEART: An intoxicating romp through the warped mind of David Lynch. Ex-con Sailor (Nicolas Cage) is wild at heart, and crazy on top. His long-suffering girlfriend (Laura Dern) bides her time as he spins his way through a revolving prison door. Wacky dream sequences and tons of cameos make this film a shoe-in for repeat viewings. Inhale pistachio cigarette here. Dir: David Lynch. C: Nicolas Cage, Laura Dern, Diane Ladd, Willem Dafoe. 1990; 125 m.

SMOKE: Smoke this! A series of vignettes suck you into a Brooklyn cigar shop, where owner Harvey Keitel spends his time philosophizing with patrons and pals. Alternately funny, wise, and sad. Dir: Wayne Wang. C: Harvey Keitel, William Hurt, Harold Perrineau Jr., Forest Whitaker. 1995; 111 m.

in your face:
LEMON MERINGUE PIE
Serves 8

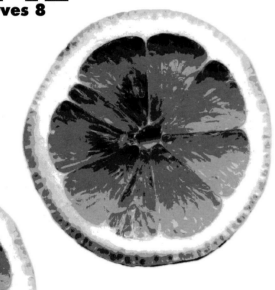

Ingredients:

(Preheat oven to 350 degrees Fahrenheit)

15 social tea biscuits
½ cup unsalted butter, melted
1 can sweetened condensed milk
3 eggs (separated into yolks and whites)
¾ cup lemon juice (fresh is best)
5 tbsp. sugar

U2 wrote a song about lemons (those Irish lads are so versatile), now you jo.
an Edge, and if you don't like it, smear it on your partner.

Method:

1) Pound biscuits into small crumbs, then mix with melted butter. Pat down into an 8" greased glass pie dish.

2) Mix can of condensed milk in a small bowl with the egg yolks and lemon juice. Beat for 3 minutes with a whisk. It will be runny.

3) Pour filling into the crust and bake for 30 minutes at 350 degrees Fahrenheit. Then remove from oven and let cool for a half hour.

4) With a whisk, whip the egg whites until foamy, then gradually add in the sugar. Beat until firm white peaks form.

5) Pour the meringue on top of the baked, cooled pie, then turn the oven on to the broil setting. Put the pie under the grill for about 30 seconds or until the meringue browns slightly.

6) Let cool for an hour before serving.

To Serve:

On its own or sided with fresh slices of kiwi fruit, this pie takes the cake.

in and add the meringue. It's simple to make, has

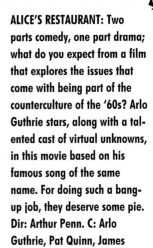

ALICE'S RESTAURANT: Two parts comedy, one part drama; what do you expect from a film that explores the issues that come with being part of the counterculture of the '60s? Arlo Guthrie stars, along with a talented cast of virtual unknowns, in this movie based on his famous song of the same name. For doing such a bang-up job, they deserve some pie. Dir: Arthur Penn. C: Arlo Guthrie, Pat Quinn, James Broderick. 1969; 111 m.

NOBODY'S FOOL: What is it about Paul Newman that's so damn appealing? I swear, in this movie he's like 100 years old, and I still want to jump his bones. Beat up, tossed out, and labeled a big zero by society, Newman finds redemption by the end of this moving comedy. And for that, he too deserves a nice piece of pie. Dir: Robert Benton. C: Paul Newman, Jessica Tandy, Melanie Griffith, Bruce Willis. 1994; 107 m.

LEMONADE JOE: A light Czech Western spoof that's full of gags and guffaws. But what, you may ask, is with the title? It seems our intrepid hero likes to guzzle the tart stuff, instead of the hard stuff. Ah, what the heck, give him a piece of pie too. Dir: Oldrich Lipsky. C: Carl Fiala, Olga Schoberova, Veta Fialova. 1967; 84 m.

let them eat

ROCKY ROAD CAKE SQUARES
Serves 12

Ingredients:

(Preheat oven to 350 degrees Fahrenheit)

¾ cup vegetable oil
2 cups sugar
2 eggs
2 ½ cups flour
¾ cup cocoa
1 tsp. baking soda
1 tsp. baking powder
½ tsp. salt
1 ½ cups cold water
1 tsp. vanilla
vegetable oil spray
1 cup milk chocolate chips
½ cup pecans, roughly chopped
½ cup minimarshmallows
vanilla ice cream
chocolate sauce

Marie Antoinette, that cheap royal, could have calmed the peasants with thi
loyal subjects, are wiser.

this:

Method:

1) In a large bowl, beat oil together with sugar, then add eggs one at a time.

2) In a medium-sized bowl, mix together flour, cocoa, baking soda, baking powder, and salt. Gradually add dry ingredients to large bowl of wet ingredients, alternating with the water. Beat well and add vanilla.

3) Spray a 9 x 13-inch Pyrex pan with vegetable oil, then pour batter into the pan and toss on an even layer of chocolate chips, pecans, and minimarshmallows.

4) Bake in the preheated 350 degree Fahrenheit oven for 45 to 50 minutes.

To Serve:

When cool, cut cake into 2-inch squares and top each piece with vanilla ice cream and chocolate sauce. Sugar highs all around!

easy-to-make chocolate confection. But you, my

BREAD AND CHOCOLATE: A goofy Italian comedy hoisted to higher ground by star Nino Manfredi's charming portrayal of a new immigrant, trying to make a go of it in Switzerland. Hmm...Switzerland. I'm thinking chocolate. Dir: Franco Brusati. C: Nino Manfredi, Anna Karina, Johnny Dorelli. 1978; 107 m.

THE CHOCOLATE WAR: Surprisingly, this picture isn't about a delicious food fight. Rather, it's a tight drama about a Catholic high-school student who refuses to take part in the annual door-to-door fundraiser. Politics and ideologies collide. Based on the book by Robert Cormier. Dir: Keith Gordon. C: John Glover, Mitchell Ilan Smith, Bud Cort, Adam Baldwin. 1988; 103 m.

WILLY WONKA AND THE CHOCOLATE FACTORY: Call the kids into the family room, this is their movie. Gene Wilder is perfectly cast as the zany "Candy Man" who allows five lucky ticket holders to have a musical tour of his chocolate factory. Alas, if they're caught with sticky fingers, they'll have to pay the consequences. Based on the book by Roald Dahl. Dir: Mel Stuart. C: Gene Wilder, Jack Albertson, Peter Ostrum. 1971; 100 m.

9½ Positions: Chocolate-Dipped Strawberries, page 158

the fat lady

ESPRESSO RICOTTA DESSERT
Serves 4

Ingredients:

1 container ricotta cheese
2 tbsp. finely ground espresso beans
1 tbsp. Kahlúa liqueur (optional)
2 tbsp. sugar
8 chocolate-covered espresso beans (for garnish)

Your friends were supposed to bring dessert but showed up empty handed. No fear; 3 ingredients, one bowl, and you're laughing.

sings:

Method:

1) In a medium-sized bowl, mix together cheese with ground espresso, Kahlúa, and sugar. Keep in fridge until using.

To Serve:

Dish out flavored cheese into nice custard cups or dessert bowls, top with two chocolate-coated beans, and serve with an Italian after-dinner liqueur, like Frangelico or Sambuca.

ce friends, but one lame-assed excuse. Have no

THE BIG CHILL: Cool treats and great beats. Probably better known for its excellent '60s soundtrack than its terrific ensemble cast, this moving drama joins a group of 7 friends as they reunite for a college friend's funeral. After dessert, turn on "Ain't Too Proud To Beg" and let your friends help you clean up like they did in the film. Dir: Lawrence Kasdan. C: William Hurt, Glenn Close, Jeff Goldblum, Tom Berenger, Kevin Kline, Mary Kay Place, Meg Tilly, JoBeth Williams. 1983; 103 m.

THE ICICLE THIEF: A highly imaginative Italian comedy in which a director (Maurizio Nichetti) is invited to introduce one of his films on network TV — and then watches in terror as his masterpiece is massacred by commercials. Very funny and telling. Dir: Maurizio Nichetti. C: Maurizio Nichetti, Caterina Labini, Heidi Komarek, Renato Scarpa. 1989; 90 m.

THE LAST SUPPER: Based on a true story, a Cuban plantation owner forces 12 of his workers to portray the Twelve Apostles at the Last Supper during the Easter festivities. Christian hypocrisy is put under the microscope and is seen as a contributing factor to the Cuban Socialist revolution. Dir: Tomas Gutierrezz Alea. C: Nelson Villagra, Silvano Rey, Lamberto Garcia, Jose Antonio Rodriguez. 1976; 110 m.

they're like

TOBLERONE CHUNK SHORTBREAD COOKIES

Makes about 3 dozen cookies

Ingredients:

(Preheat oven to 325 degrees Fahrenheit)

1 cup unsalted butter, softened
½ cup packed brown sugar
½ tsp. vanilla extract
2 ½ cups all-purpose flour
2 regular-sized Toblerone bars, roughly chopped into large chunks

THESE COOKIES MAKE GREAT GIFTS DURING THE HOLIDAYS. WHEN COMPLETELY COOLED, LINE A SMALL BOX OR TIN WITH TISSUE PAPER, DROP IN AS MANY COOKIES AS YOU'RE WILLING TO SPARE, THEN CLOSE IT UP AND WRAP WITH RIBBON AND A HOMEMADE CARD. HOW VERY MARTHAESQUE.

Can we tawk cookies? These little shortbread dumplings should be illegal – cookie melts in your mouth, then the chocolate melts in your hands, and fin

buttah:

Method:

1) In a medium bowl, cream butter and sugar together with a wooden spoon, until it becomes light and fluffy (this will take several minutes of heavy breathing, er, beating).

2) Stir in vanilla, then gradually mix in flour, constantly stirring, until the dough can be formed into a stiff ball. Add more flour if sticky.

3) Using a rolling pin (or a round bottle or jar), roll out the dough on a lightly floured surface. If you have a cookie cutter, cut out as many cookies as you can get out of the sheet of dough, or, using a serrated knife, cut the sheet of dough into even 1 ½" squares.

4) Arrange cookies a couple of inches apart on ungreased cookie sheets. Then, using your thumb, make a light imprint in the center of each cookie and place a chunk of Toblerone in the dent.

5) Bake in a preheated 325 degree Fahrenheit oven for 10 to 15 minutes, or until lightly browned. Cool on wire racks.

To Serve:

A big glass of milk helps 'em go down nice and smooth.

ut they're not, so eat people, eat! First the buttery lly, you melt into your chair. Nuff said.

A CHRISTMAS STORY: I catch this knee-slapper every Christmas. Set in the 1940s, all that our bespectacled protagonist wants from this world is a Red Ryder BB gun. The only problem is, if he gets one, he may put his eye out. A hilarious family comedy. Dir: Bob Clark. C: Peter Billingsley, Darren McGavin, Melinda Dillon. 1983; 98 m.

THE BISCUIT EATER: An excellent film that the whole family can enjoy. A white boy and a black boy become the best of friends as they pick the runt of a litter to raise as a champion bird dog. Bake up some cookies, pour the milk, and let the kids enjoy this timeless beauty. Dir: Stuart Heisler. C: Billy Lee, Cordell Hickman, Helene Millard. 1940; 83 m.

IT'S A WONDERFUL LIFE: This is my pick for best Christmas picture. Down-on-his-luck James Stewart contemplates suicide, and it takes an angel (Henry Travers) to show him what an impact his life has made on his town. The all-star cast shines, and the humor remains as fresh as a warm cookie. Dir: Frank Capra. C: James Stewart, Donna Reed, Lionel Barrymore, Thomas Mitchell, Henry Travers. 1946; 129 m.

LEMON POPPY SEED CAKE
Serves 9

Ingredients:

(Preheat oven to 350 degrees Fahrenheit)

3 eggs, beaten
1 ¼ cups sugar
½ cup butter, melted
1 tsp. vanilla extract
½ cup fresh lemon juice
2 tsp. baking powder
2 cups flour
3 tbsp. poppy seeds
vegetable oil spray

**In The Wizard of Oz, wistful Dorothy fell asleep in a field of poppies. You be
too much lemon cake?**

as anymore:

Method:

1) In a large bowl, mix together the beaten eggs, sugar, melted butter, vanilla, and lemon juice.

2) In a smaller bowl, mix the baking powder in with the flour. Be sure it's well blended, then stir in the poppy seeds.

3) Slowly stir the flour mixture in with the wet ingredients, then beat together.

4) Spray a 7 x 11-inch baking pan with vegetable oil, then pour in batter. Bake in the preheated 350 degree Fahrenheit oven for 45 minutes.

To Serve:

Cut into large squares and serve with a side of sorbet and a cup of tea. Simply charming.

the judge: Was she stoned, or did she simply eat

THE BAKER'S WIFE: In this classic French comedy, a gifted baker decides to stop creating his culinary treats until his philandering wife is returned to his bed. The town folk, starved for fresh bread, take it upon themselves to see that the baker is appeased. Dir: Marcel Pagnol. C: Raimu, Ginette Leclerc, Charles Moulin. 1938;124 m.

THE FABULOUS BAKER BOYS: All right, so they may be Bakers in name only, but as if they wouldn't love this delectable poppy-seed cake. A piano-playing brother lounge act hires a charismatic female vocalist to spruce up their tawdry show. She gets very friendly with the better-looking brother, and tensions rise a la John and Yoko. Dir: Steve Kloves. C: Jeff Bridges, Michelle Pfeiffer, Beau Bridges. 1989; 116 m.

MONTY PYTHON'S THE MEANING OF LIFE: A loopy series of sketch-comedy bits linked thematically by the cycle of life. Pop it in the VCR for the knee-slapping humor, but stay tuned for the restaurant vomit skit, which is so funny, it just might make you — you guessed it — puke. Eat after the movie; this cake is too good to waste. Dir: Terry Jones. C: Graham Chapman, John Cleese, Terry Gilliam, Eric Idle, Michael Palin. 1983; 107 m.

breakfast

all hot an b

BAGEL SPREADS
Each recipe makes ¼ lb.

Ingredients:

Method:

Mixed Herb

Mix together ¼ lb. softened butter with 1 tbsp. lemon juice, 2 tbsp. chopped chives, 1 tbsp. chopped parsley, 1 tbsp. chopped basil, and salt and pepper to taste. Spread into a tubular shape on tinfoil and roll into a tight 1 ½-inch log. Put in freezer and slice off ¼-inch rounds as needed.

Garlic Onion

Mix together ¼ lb. softened butter with 1 tbsp. lemon juice, 1 minced garlic clove, 2 chopped green onions, 1 tbsp. chopped parsley, and salt and pepper to taste. Spread into a tubular shape on tinfoil and roll into a tight 1 ½-inch log. Put in freezer and slice off ¼-inch rounds as needed.

Slept through the alarm as usual? With these yummy spreads standing by, y unless you forgot to buy bagels, in which case, I can't help you.

uttered:

Cinnamon Brown Sugar

Mix together ¼ lb. softened butter with 1 tbsp. brown sugar, 1 tsp. cinnamon, and ¼ tsp. vanilla. Spread into a tubular shape on tinfoil and roll into a tight 1 ½-inch log. Put in freezer and slice off ¼-inch rounds as needed.

Veggie Cream Cheese

Mix together ¼ lb. cream cheese with 2 tbsp. minced red pepper, 2 tbsp. grated carrot, 1 chopped green onion, 4 chopped green olives, a ¼ tsp. chili flakes, and salt to taste. Spread into a little bowl and keep covered in the fridge until serving.

Salmon Spread

Mix together ¼ lb. cream cheese with 2 tbsp. softened butter, 1 oz. minced lox or smoked salmon, 1 tbsp. lemon juice, 1 chopped green onion, and salt and pepper to taste. Spread into a little bowl and keep covered in the fridge until serving.

u'll never have to skip breakfast again. That is,

BREAD, LOVE AND DREAMS: Before he became a big-time film director, Vittorio De Sica was a matinee idol in Italy — looks and brains! Here he plays a hunky guy being chased by an aggressive woman. Fun stuff. Dir: Luigi Comencini. C: Vittorio De Sica, Gina Lollobrigida. 1954; 90 m.

DELICATESSEN: An innovative French black comedy set in a sepia-toned post-apocalyptic world. Our protagonist, a former circus clown, comes to town to take on a job as a butcher's assistant. He makes friends, dates a girl, and is well fed. But what he doesn't realize is that it will soon be time to restock the meat shelves and put another ad in the "help wanted" section. Dir: Marc Caro, Jean-Pierre Jeunet. C: Marie-Laure Dougnac, Dominique Pinon, Karin Viard. 1991; 95 m.

THE PHILADELPHIA STORY: A stellar cast dishes out the laughs in this perfect comedy about high society. Headstrong bride-to-be Katharine Hepburn has cold feet, but her family will see to it that those chilly toes go marching down the aisle come hell or high water. James Stewart won a best actor Oscar for his hilarious turn. Dir: George Cukor. C: Cary Grant, Katharine Hepburn, James Stewart, Ruth Hussey. 1940; 112 m.

PEANUT BUTTER AND BANANA FRENCH TOAST

Serves 2

Ingredients:

¼ cup cool water
½ tsp. vanilla extract
3 eggs, beaten
2 tsp. peanut butter
4 slices egg bread (challah)
1 tbsp. margarine
2 bananas, peeled and sliced into ½-inch chunks (some reserved for garnish)
2 tbsp. real maple syrup

French toast, sleep-ins, maple syrup, and Saturday morning c
Really.

Method:

1) In a shallow bowl (like a soup bowl) beat water and vanilla in with eggs until well mixed.

2) Spread a tsp. of peanut butter on two slices of the bread and dip them in the egg mixture. Then take the other two slices and dip them in the egg mixture. Heat margarine in a large frying pan over medium-high heat, and when margarine starts to bubble, add the peanut butter slices, peanut butter side up. Quickly lay out banana pieces onto the peanut butter and top with a slice of egg-dipped bread. Squish the sandwich together with a spatula.

3) Let cook for about 3 minutes on the first side, then flip and cook for another few minutes on the other side. After 6 or 7 minutes of cooking, if it seems too moist, cover pan with a lid and let cook an additional minute or 2.

To Serve:

Turn out the French toast sandwiches onto big plates, top with a few thoughtfully placed banana slices, then pour the maple syrup over top. Ooey, gooey good.

artoons – this is what life was meant to be.

BANANAS: This is Woody Allen doing what he does best – being the nebbish, klutzy, self-absorbed neurotic guy whom we all love or love to hate. Here he gets into trouble trying to impress a woman. He becomes a political activist to get close to her and inadvertently winds up the dictator of a banana republic. Dir: Woody Allen. C: Woody Allen, Louise Lasser, Carlos Montalban, Howard Cosell. 1971; 82 m.

THE BIG SLEEP: Wake up and watch this moody crime film. Detective Philip Marlowe (Humphrey Bogart) investigates a murder while falling for seductress Lauren Bacall. Some nice dark humor permeates, in this, a classic of its genre. Dir: Howard Hawks. C: Humphrey Bogart, Lauren Bacall, John Ridgely, Martha Vickers. 1946; 114 m.

BREAKFAST AT TIFFANY'S: Audrey Hepburn is at her trendsetting best as she plays an out-of-control party girl/personal escort, in this offbeat winner. The film is part love story, part comedy, and all fun with the cool costumes and perfect Henry Mancini score. Dir: Blake Edwards. C: Audrey Hepburn, George Peppard, Patricia Neal, Buddy Ebsen. 1961; 115 m.

the java-free
MUESLI WITH FRUIT
Serves 1

Ingredients:

1 cup mixed seasonal fruit (assorted berries, bananas, apples, pineapples, orange sections, pears, nectarines, etc.)
1 cup plain low-fat yogurt
½ cup muesli (a cereal found in health food stores)
1 tsp. honey
1 tbsp. slivered almonds (toasted)

To TOAST ALMONDS, SPREAD NUTS OUT EVENLY ON A COOKIE SHEET AND BAKE IN A PREHEATED OVEN AT 350° FAHRENHEIT FOR 7 MINUTES. KEEP A WATCHFUL EYE ON THEM BECAUSE THEY BURN EASILY.

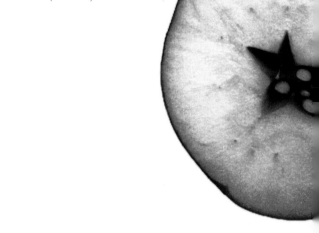

How do you think those hard-bodied aerobics instructors keep pumping after coffee beans that is. Fast, simple, cheap – and hey, lose a few off your rump

kick-start:

Method:

1) Wash and cut mixed fruit into bite-sized pieces.

2) Add the prepared fruit to a big cereal bowl, then the yogurt and the muesli. Drizzle with honey, then sprinkle on the toasted almonds to top it all off.

To Serve:

Hunker down at the table, open up the morning paper, and dig in.

**five classes? They use the boost without beans –
too.**

knock knock. wh omelet me in:

OMELETS THREE WAYS
Serves 2

Ingredients:

Method:

Basic Omelets

In a small bowl whisk together 4 eggs with 2 tbsp. of cold water. Heat ½ tbsp. of butter in a large frying pan on medium heat, and when butter turns golden in color, pour in half of the egg mixture. Cook for about 2 minutes, then fold one side in a third of the way. Cook a while longer, add salt and pepper to taste, then roll out of pan so that it lands bottom side up on the plate. Repeat with the other ½ tbsp. of butter and remaining egg mixture.

French Herb Omelets

In a small bowl, whisk together 4 eggs with 2 tbsp. of cold

You know that age-old question: Which came first; the chicken or the egg? I on this one. As for the omelets, here are a few basic suggestions but be inno

o's there?

water, 1 tsp. chopped parsley, 1 tsp. chopped tarragon, and 1 tsp. chopped chives. Heat ½ tbsp. of butter in a large frying pan on medium heat, and when butter turns golden in color, pour in half of the egg mixture. Cook for about 2 minutes, then fold one side in a third of the way. Cook a while longer, add salt and pepper to taste, then roll out of pan so that it lands bottom side up on the plate. Repeat with the other ½ tbsp. of butter and remaining egg mixture.

Spinach And Monterey Jack Cheese Omelets

Rinse and dry 2 cups of fresh spinach, remove stems, then wilt spinach in a tsp. of butter in a frying pan. Remove from pan and set aside. In a small bowl, whisk together 4 eggs with 2 tbsp. of cold water. Heat ½ tbsp. of butter in a large frying pan on medium heat, and when butter turns golden in color, pour in half of the egg mixture. Cook for 1 minute, spread ½ the cooked spinach over top, then splotch with ¼ cup of grated Monterey Jack cheese, and cook for another minute. Fold one side of the omelet in a third of the way, cook a while longer, add salt and pepper to taste, then roll out of pan so that it lands bottom side up on the plate. Repeat with the other ½ tbsp. of butter and remaining egg mixture, spinach, and cheese.

know the answer. It was the chicken. Just trust me vative and create your own eggstravaganza.

THE EGG AND I: A folksy old comedy based on the best-seller by Betty MacDonald. A wealthy Park Avenue madam gets talked into moving to the country to raise chickens with her nature-loving hubby. Extra-special performances by Ma and Pa Kettle meant a future film series to call their own. Dir: Chester Erskine. C: Claudette Cobert, Fred MacMurray, Marjorie Main, Percy Kilbride. 1947; 108 m.

PILLOW TALK: Rock Hudson and Doris Day play the battle of the sexes in this flashy, fun comedy. The sets and costumes are almost as dazzling as the stars' pearly whites, but this show isn't just a pretty face; it won Oscars for its story and screenplay. Dir: Michael Gordon. C: Doris Day, Rock Hudson, Tony Randall, Thelma Ritter. 1959; 102 m.

SABRINA: Classy as ever, Audrey Hepburn plays the title role as the offspring of a chauffeur to a wealthy family. After spending many years in Paris, the beguiling Hepburn returns and is pursued by two charming men. While in Paris, Sabrina attends Le Cordon Bleu cooking school, where she has some trouble mastering the omelet. Dir: Billy Wilder. C: Humphrey Bogart, Audrey Hepburn, William Holden. 1954; 113 m.

CHOCOLATE CHIP PANCAKES
Makes 12 big pancakes

Ingredients:

1 ½ cups flour
½ tsp. salt
3 tbsp. sugar
1 ½ tsp. baking powder
1 cup milk chocolate chips*
1 egg, beaten
3 tbsp. butter, melted
1 ¼ cups milk
vegetable oil
real maple syrup

*Believe it or not, some people aren't huge chocolate fans. The chips can be substituted with blueberries, raspberries, sliced strawberries, bananas, or a combination of these fruits.

I took a little trip back in time and discovered this favorite Sunday morning would dream of chocolate chip pancakes. And now my fantasy comes true.

house rock:

Method:

1) In a medium-sized bowl, mix together the dry ingredients. Set aside. In a smaller bowl, combine wet ingredients and mix well. Then, slowly mix the wet ingredients in with the dry ones. Stir together until combined. It will be slightly lumpy. Set aside for an hour.

2) Drop 2 tbsp. of oil into a large frying pan and heat on medium. When hot, pour a big spoonful of batter into the pan (you can cook 2 or 3 pancakes at a time). When bubbles appear on the surface, check underneath pancakes with a spatula. Once they are golden brown, flip over and cook until other side is browned. Keep the batter flowing and add more oil as needed.

To Serve:

Stack the hotcakes and place a bottle of maple syrup on the table. Then let the little piggies help themselves to as many pancakes as they can muster.

treat. High on Froot Loops and Captain Crunch, I

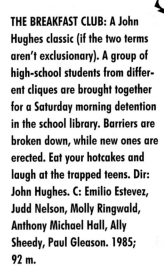

THE BREAKFAST CLUB: A John Hughes classic (if the two terms aren't exclusionary). A group of high-school students from different cliques are brought together for a Saturday morning detention in the school library. Barriers are broken down, while new ones are erected. Eat your hotcakes and laugh at the trapped teens. Dir: John Hughes. C: Emilio Estevez, Judd Nelson, Molly Ringwald, Anthony Michael Hall, Ally Sheedy, Paul Gleason. 1985; 92 m.

FERRIS BUELLER'S DAY OFF: Is there any day more perfect than the one Ferris Bueller, his girlfriend, and his best friend had when they ditched school for a day of amusement? I don't think so, unless they had chocolate chip pancakes before all the excitement began. Dir: John Hughes. C: Matthew Broderick, Alan Ruck, Mia Sara, Jeffrey Jones, Edie McClurg. 1986; 103 m.

THE PAJAMA GAME: This toe-tapping musical, from the Broadway hit, is about union woes at a pajama factory. A romantic comedy full of song and dance, it will wake up even the heaviest of sleepers. And if it doesn't, the aroma of fresh-brewed coffee and piping hot pancakes will. Dir: George Abbott, Stanley Donen. C: Doris Day, John Raitt, Carol Haney, Eddie Foy Jr., Reta Shaw. 1957; 101 m.

courtesy of Daphne McAfee

cocktails

I'll drink to t

SETTING UP A BAR AND MAKING COCKTAILS

The Bar

Stocking your bar doesn't have to be a major investment. Buy several bottles of the basics (ask traveling friends to get you duty-free booze), a few utensils (often found at yard sales and second-hand stores at bargain prices), some fresh fruit, ice, and coasters. I got most of my drink information from a 25¢ pocket book from the '60s that I stole from my parent's bar. The pages may be yellowed, but the recipes never change.

The Equipment

1 water pitcher
1 double-ended jigger
1 pitcher for mixing

a large variety of glasses
1 shaker with two containers – one for ice, one for ingredients
1 long stirrer, like a wooden spoon
1 shaker strainer
1 measuring cup
1 measuring spoon set
1 bottle opener
1 corkscrew
1 ice bucket
1 ice tongs
1 small chopping board
1 small sharp knife
1 juicer
1 hand blender
1 vegetable peeler
toothpicks
coasters

cocktail napkins
straws – short and long
tiny umbrellas and stirrers (optional but fun)

The Booze and Mixers

You can keep as much or as little liquor on hand as you please. It takes years to build up your stock, most of it usually arriving as gifts. Here are some suggestions for the basics to a wide range of drinks:

a bottle each of Scotch, whiskey, gin, dry vermouth, sherry, vodka, rum, and brandy

a bottle each of soda water, tonic water, Coke, 7-Up, Ginger Ale, and angostura bitters

Cocktails and lounge culture are swinging back into fashion big time. Beer a tough day of job searching. Set up your own little bar, take orders from you full-on retro effect.

that:

a jar of maraschino cherries, a jar of pimento stuffed olives, a jar of cocktail onions, Tabasco sauce, Worcestershire sauce, sugar, fresh lemons, oranges, and limes
loads of ice

the drinks

(Each recipe makes 1 beverage)

On The Rocks

Ingredients:

1 ½ oz. liquor
3 ice cubes

Method:

Pour liquor over ice in a short glass. A twist of lemon can be added if desired.

Highball

Ingredients:

3 ice cubes
1 ½ oz. liquor
mixer

Method:

Drop ice cubes into a tall glass, then add liquor to ice. Fill about ⅔ with a mixer (e.g., water, Coke, soda water) and stir gently.

Martini

Ingredients:

½ oz. dry vermouth
3 ice cubes
2 oz. gin
3 olives
1 toothpick

Method:

Mix vermouth and ice together in a pitcher. Add gin, stir, and strain into a chilled martini glass. Poke olives onto toothpick and drop into glass. A lemon twist can be substituted for the olives.

Orange Blossom

Ingredients:

1 ½ oz. gin
½ oz. orange juice
½ tsp. sugar
squirt of lime juice
chopped ice

Method:

Shake the ingredients with chopped ice and strain into a chilled cocktail glass. An orange twist and an umbrella and straw are nice touches.

d wine are fine, but nothing beats a nice cocktail or tall beverage after a guests, and make sure to have plenty of sexist napkins standing by for that

MANHATTAN
1 WHISKY
1 SHARE VERMOUTH
DASH ANGOSTURA BITTERS
STIR WITH CRACKED ICE
STRAIN SERVE WITH
CHERRY

WHISKEY
SOUR
2 OZ. WHISKEY
1 TSP. POWDERED S
JUICE ½ LEMON & ½ L
SHAKE WITH CRACKED
STRAIN AND SERVE

VODKA
COLLINS
1 JIGGER VODKA
JUICE ½ LEMON
1 TSP. SUGAR
POUR OVER CUBES STIR
CHERRY & LEMON SLICE

Martini, page 195

Bloody Mary

Ingredients:

1 ½ oz. vodka
3 oz. tomato juice
½ oz. fresh lemon juice
chopped ice
dash of Worcestershire sauce
dash of Tabasco sauce
shake of salt and pepper
a celery stick

Method:

Shake first 3 ingredients together with ice, then strain into a tall glass. Mix in remaining seasonings and garnish with the celery stick.

Black Russian

Ingredients:

2 oz. vodka
1 oz. Kahlúa
3 ice cubes

Method:

Pour ingredients over a few ice cubes in a short glass and stir well.

Manhattan

Ingredients:

1 ½ oz. whiskey
½ oz. sweet vermouth
dash of angostura bitters
ice cubes
1 maraschino cherry

Method:

Shake first 3 ingredients with ice cubes, then strain into a chilled cocktail glass. Drop in the cherry for garnish.

Whiskey Sour

Ingredients:

1 ½ oz. lemon juice
½ tsp. sugar
1 ½ oz. whiskey
1 maraschino cherry
chopped ice

Method:

Shake the first 3 ingredients with chopped ice, and strain into a short glass. Garnish with a cherry.

Daiquiri

Ingredients:

½ tsp. sugar
½ oz. lime juice
1 ½ oz. white rum
chopped ice
lime wedge

hat

Method:

Shake first 3 ingredients together with ice and strain into a chilled cocktail glass. Garnish with lime.

Margarita

Ingredients:

½ oz. lime juice
½ tsp. sugar
1 ½ oz. tequila
chopped ice
lime wedge
salt

Method:

Shake lime juice, sugar, and tequila together with ice. Rub rim of a chilled cocktail glass with lime wedge, then dip in salt. Strain drink into glass and garnish with lime wedge.

Singapore Sling

Ingredients:

½ tsp. sugar
1 lime, juiced
¾ oz. kirsch
2 oz. gin
dash of angostura bitters
chopped ice
4 ice cubes
soda water
1 maraschino cherry
1 lime wedge
1 orange slice

Method:

Shake together the first 6 ingredients, then strain over ice cubes into a tall glass. Fill with soda water and garnish with fruit, a long straw, and an umbrella.

Tom Collins

Ingredients:

juice of 1/2 a lemon
1/2 tsp. sugar
chopped ice
1 1/2 oz. gin
soda water
lemon wedge
maraschino cherry

Method:

Shake together lemon and sugar with ice. Stir in the gin, then pour into a tall glass. Add soda water, lemon wedge, and cherry.

Screwdriver

Ingredients:

1 ½ oz. vodka
3 ice cubes
orange juice

Method:

In a tall glass, pour vodka over ice cubes. Fill with orange juice and gently stir.

Greyhound

Ingredients:

1 ½ oz. vodka
3 ice cubes
grapefruit juice

Method:

In a tall glass, pour vodka over ice cubes. Fill with grapefruit juice and gently stir.

Mint Julep

Ingredients:

3 fresh mint sprigs
1 tsp. sugar
1 tsp. water
shaved ice
1 ½ oz. + ½ oz. bourbon

Method:

Chop up the mint, then stir together with sugar and water in a tall glass. Fill the glass with shaved ice, then add 1 ½ oz. of bourbon and stir until the glass becomes frosted. Add remaining ½ oz. of bourbon, drop in a straw, stir, and garnish with another sprig of mint.

Spritzer

Ingredients:

3 oz. white wine
soda water

Method:

To a large wine glass add chilled wine and soda water.

wine basics

Now that you've done all the cooking, your guests want wine too? Yes, I know, it never ends. Wine tasting is a mysterious, complicated art that many boring snobs spend years learning. You don't have to. The basic wine dilemmas go like this: Red or white? Domestic or imported? Expensive or cheap? Basically, it's all a matter of taste. Here's a miniguide to vino jargon that will give you that glazed look of sophistication without becoming drunk on the details of expertise.

that

Essential Tips to Impress Friends:

Bacchus was the Greek god of wine, who held the kind of orgies you just don't hear about anymore.

For all the hype, wine is just grape juice with added yeast that enables its natural sugars to ferment into alcohol.

Wines are divided into several categories that sound pretty foreign – well, they are foreign.
Reds: Cabernet Sauvignon, Merlot, Pinot Noir, Zinfandel, Beaujolais, and Chianti.
Whites: Chardonnay, Sauvignon Blanc, Riesling, and Pinot Blanc.

These names either refer to the grapes the wines are made from, like Merlot and Chardonnay, or the region in which the wines were made, like Chianti in Italy. Just to confuse you, some wines have whimsical names given by individual winemakers, but I don't want to talk about them. (Let them pay the price for being rebels.) The general rule is this: Wines from the U.S., Australia, South Africa, New Zealand, Chile, and Argentina are usually named for grapes, while European wines are often named for wine regions – think of France's Burgundy and Bordeaux. The more information on the label, the better. The label will give the origin of the grapes (if you can get the exact district or vineyard where the wine was prepared, it's a bonus), the vintage (or year), and the alcohol level.

The golden rule for people too lazy to read about wine but still wanting to impress people: Avoid screw-on caps.

Even though the trend these days is that every wine goes with every food, it's not really true. White wine usually goes best with fish, vegetables, and white meats, and red wine suits red meats. Of course there are exceptions, and you should know when to break the rules. Often grilled fish, or meatier varieties like tuna, go better with red wine, as do spicy or tomato-based veggie dishes. And since chicken can be prepared in a cornucopia of ways, chicken/wine matches will come from the intensity of the poultry's added flavorings. Grilled chicken goes well with whites or a light-bodied red, and spicy foods can go with anything from a powerful white to a nice Zinfandel.

Wine prices range from $5 to thousands of dollars. What's the deal? Well, often more expensive wines are made from better grapes, coming from smaller, richer crops. In addition, aging wine in oak barrels, for instance, can be pricey because of the cost of the barrels and time. Finally, scarcity can put the cost of a good vintage over the moon. A lot of that has to do with snob appeal because there's just no way that a $600 bottle is 60 times better than a $10 corker.

Becoming a Wine Connoisseur:

There are 4 points to consider when tasting wine: color, smell, taste, and finish.
First we'll talk color. Take a proper wine glass (or an empty jam jar) and fill it up a quarter of the way with wine. Tip it up toward a light to check for clarity. If it's cloudy, the wine was poorly made. A rich color is a good sign, whereas a weak color can point toward a lackluster flavor.
Now for smell. Swoosh the wine

around in the glass to release the wine's aroma. Once the wine settles, there will be a thin coating that clings to the walls of the glass. As it evaporates, it will give off a smell that will emanate an aroma. The aroma is the various scents the wine gives off, like lemon, strawberry, and peachy smells. There can also be winemaker-added scents like oak, cedar, or even vanilla. If you happened to be blessed with a heightened sense of smell, now's the time to impress your peers.

As for taste, balance is the most important element. There must be a good working relationship between the sweetness of fruit and the zinginess of acid. The wine should taste good, deli-cious even, not harsh or bland. When you take a swig of wine, swoosh it around in your mouth. Let it roll over your tongue and through your cheeks. You'll sense different flavors as the wine hits various parts of your tongue: sweetness at the front, bitterness at the back, and acidity along the sides.

Now for the big finish. It's time to swallow! If your wine tastes like battery acid, spit it out and try your luck with another bottle. If you've enjoyed the first gulp, close your mouth and breath slowly through your nose for a few seconds. How is the aftertaste? You may be surprised as some great wines have a burst of new flavors for an exciting kick at the end.

Here is a List of Recommended Wines:

Cheap Whites:
Chardonnay
1994 The Monterey Vineyard, California
1995 Fortant de France, France
1994 Napa Ridge, Central Coast
1995 Drostdy-Hof, South Africa
Sauvignon Blanc
1994 Napa Ridge, North Coast
1994 Fortant de France, France
1995 Fetzer Fume Blanc, California

Cheap Reds:
Cabernet Sauvignon
1992 Vina Undurraga, Chile
1993 Canyon Road, California
Merlot
1996 Montes, Chile
1995 Carmen, Chile
Pinot Noir
1995 Napa Ridge, California
1992 Pedroncelli Winery, California
Zinfandel
1996 Robert Mondavi, Woodbridge,
California
1995 Sutter Home, California

For a Little Bit More:

Whites:
Chardonnay
1993 Ernest & Julio Gall-Sonoma
Winery, Sonoma
1996 Cousino-Macul, Chili
Others
1996 Hippo Creek, South Africa
1995 Verdicchio, Italy
1994 Macon Villages, France

Reds:
Cabernet Sauvignon
1992 Sebastiani Vineyards, Sonoma
1992 Wynns, Coonawarra, Australia
Chianti Classico
1993 Toscolo, Italy
1995 Aziano, Italy
1995 Brolio, Italy
Pinot Noir
1993 Louis Latour, French
1993 Maison Louis Jadot, France
Zinfandel
1993 Baron Herzog Wine Cellars,
California

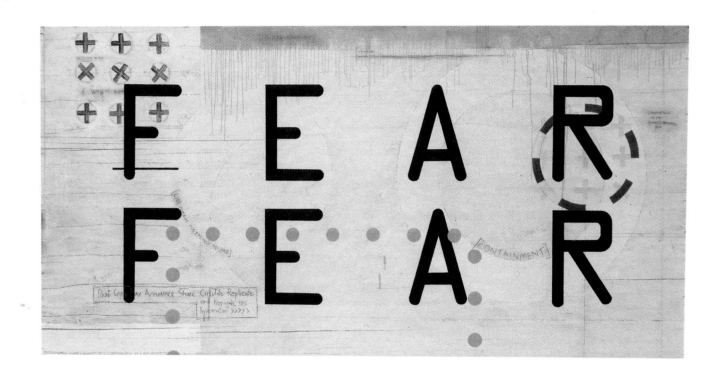

courtesy of Eden Robbins

foodstuff

BASIC COOKING TERMS

Baste: To spoon liquid over food while it cooks, adding flavoring and preventing drying

Beat: To mix with a fast, smooth motion that lifts mixture over and over, introducing air

Boil: To cook in steaming liquid in which the bubbles break at the surface

Chop: To cut into fine, medium, or coarse pieces with a sharp knife

Dough: A mixture of dry and wet ingredients which is stiff enough to be handled

Dredge: To coat with flour

Fillet: A long, thin boneless strip of fish or meat

Fold in: To cut through the center of a mixture with a large spoon and combine the mixture from the bottom to the top, repeating until airy but blended

Garnish: To decorate the prepared food

Julienne: To cut food into matchlike strips

Knead: To work dough with a pressing motion, accompanied by folding and stretching

Mince: To cut or chop food into very fine pieces

Pareve: Food containing neither milk nor meat products (like pareve chicken soup base)

Poach: To cover with and cook in simmering liquid, allowing food to retain its shape

Puree: To process food, making a smooth, thick mixture

Simmer: To cook at a temperature that is just below the boiling point

Stock: The base to most soups, coming from the liquid in which meat, fish, or vegetables have been cooked. Also available in a powder form that you add to water.

Whip: To beat rapidly, increasing volume by the incorporation of air

You're new in the kitchen and ready to go ahead whole hog, but some of the cooking terms have you scratching your head in wonder. Here's a list of som terms, along with brief explanations.

nat mean?

METRIC CONVERSION

For convenience the conversion from imperial to metric measures has been rounded off into units of 25 grams. See table below for recommended equivalents. Never mix metric and imperial measures in one recipe. Always use level measures.

Dry Measures

Imperial	Recommended Metric Conversion
1 oz.	25 g.
2 oz.	50 g.
3 oz.	75 g.
4 oz.	100 g.
12 oz.	350 g.
16 oz. (1 lb.)	450 g.
20 oz. (1 ¼ lb.)	575 g.
2 lb. 3 oz.	1,000 g. (1 kg.)

Liquid or Volume Measures

Imperial	Recommended Metric Conversion
½ tsp.	2 ml.
1 tsp.	5 ml.
1 tbsp.	15 ml.
1 fl. oz. (2 tbsp.)	30 ml.
2 fl. oz.	50 ml.
5 fl. oz. (¼ pt.)	150 ml.
1/2 pt.	300 ml.
1 pt.	600 ml.
1 ¾ pt.	1,000 ml. (1 liter)

perplexing common

hardware:
WHAT YOU'LL NEED TO EQUIP YOUR KITCHEN

You don't have to go out and buy all of this stuff at once; just build up your supplies little by little. I was able to get along nicely for 2 years with just one pot, a wok, a kettle, and a $1 knife. Of course, I did eat out a lot.

2 saucepans with covers: one large one (3 quarts) and a smaller one (1 ½ quarts)

2 nonstick frying pans: one large one (10 to 12 inches) and a small one (7 to 8 inches)

1 big pasta/soup pot (8 quarts)

1 wok: nonstick or regular (if you usually cook for just you and a roomie, buy a small one, but if you regularly turn out full-fledged feasts, buy the next size up)

1 kettle: for boiling water for recipes, tea, or instant coffee

1 set of measuring cups

1 set of measuring spoons

1 large measuring pitcher: for mixing drinks, soups, dressings, and sauces

1 set of 3 mixing bowls: small, medium, and large

one 8- or 9-inch baking pan: Pyrex is best

one 7 x 11-inch baking dish

one 9 x 5 x 3-inch loaf pan

one 9-inch pie pan

1 cake rack

2 nonstick cookie sheets

1 spatula

1 wire whisk

1 soup ladle

1 large stirring spoon

1 slatted stirring spoon

1 long wooden spoon

1 cutting board: the bigger, the better

1 chef's knife: knife prices range from $1 to hundreds of dollars. Buy the best you can afford.

1 smaller serrated knife

1 grater

1 vegetable peeler

1 can opener

1 bottle opener: Not too necessary these days, but you never know.

1 corkscrew: Buy a good solid one. You'll use it often.

one 1-inch pastry brush: for brushing butter or egg washes over baked goods

2 colanders: a large one and a small one, for draining pasta to rinsing berries

1 hand blender: I have a 5-speed Braun, and I love it.

1 perforated 12-inch pizza pan: a must for crisp crust

2 ice cube trays

2 dish towels (minimum)

1 pair oven mitts

STOCKING YOUR CUPBOARDS AND FRIDGE

You're new to the cooking game and aren't sure what to have around the kitchen to make it work for you. With this list, along with freshly bought fruits, vegetables, nuts, meats, and seafood, you can make just about every recipe in this book from start to finish. Honest.

Baking Needs:

chocolate chips
unsalted butter
sugar
eggs
milk
honey
cocoa powder
ground cinnamon
brown sugar
cornstarch
vanilla extract

flour
baking powder
baking soda
cornmeal

Oils, Vinegars, And Condiments:

vegetable oil
olive oil
Tabasco sauce
margarine
Worcestershire sauce
vegetable oil spray (like Pam)
sesame oil
red wine vinegar
white vinegar
balsamic vinegar
Dijon mustard
soy sauce
ketchup
mayonnaise

Herbs And Spices:

dried cumin
curry powder
cayenne pepper
salt
garlic powder
paprika
black pepper
dried oregano
mustard powder
chili flakes
dried basil
bay leafs
ginger powder

pping list:

Miscellaneous:

red lentils
rice
cooking onions
canned tomatoes
tomato paste
fresh garlic
fresh ginger
canned chickpeas
fresh lemons
breadcrumbs
all-purpose potatoes
pareve soup mix (vegetarian soup base,
vegetable or chicken flavor)
bottled artichokes
bottled roasted red pepper
peanut butter
couscous
dry pasta
coffee
tea
canned tuna

cold cereal
crackers
real maple syrup
popcorn
juice
soda pop
Parmesan cheese
apples

Cleaning Supplies And Kitchen Helpers:

all-purpose cleaning spray
tinfoil
pot-scrubbing pads
liquid dish detergent
sandwich bags
matches
candles
napkins
hand soap

paper towels
plastic wrap
small fire extinguisher
sponges
trash bags
toothpicks

thanks

Evan Solomon: for assuring me that I could write a book and then helping me through the entire process.

Malcolm Brown: for donating his time and effort to the initial proposal and allowing his art to become the hippest part of the book.

Doug O'Neill: for reviewing the recipes and adding a few zesty touches of his own.

Nick Pitt: for understanding my whacky concept right away and giving me a book deal. There should be more publishers like him.

Additional thanks to the following people, places, and things: everyone at Warwick Publishing, John Carron for his legal expertise, Erin for looking over the movie blurbs, enthusiastic family and friends including Bubi Fran, Boobie Ronnie, my brothers and their spouses, the Chabibis, the people at Shift, Ilona, Shrug, Anna, Tammi, Naomi, and Lorraine. In addition, I couldn't have done this without my parents' kitchen, my Macintosh PowerBook and ink-jet printer, my trusty Cordon Bleu chef's cap, the VCR, the Internet, Coca-Cola, chocolate, microwavable popcorn, bananas, fresh herbs and spices, Beck, Tracy Bonham, Counting Crows, and Canada, my home and native land.

Malcolm Brown

Born in England, Malcolm Brown (front cover design and original artwork) has worked commercially as an art director and graphic designer for over ten years. Combining text and image in his paintings, he plays with the aesthetic and makes fun of the concerns of commercial design. His paintings affront rather than soothe, and are ironic rather than earnest. Brown works on plywood with a variety of materials, paint, photographs, and found objects, and the dimensions are often unusual which forces some paintings to be read like signs. He is currently the art director of Shift magazine in Toronto, and can be contacted at m@shift.com for more information on his most recent work.

Bill Milne

Originally from Toronto, Bill Milne (cover photograph & colour food photography) studied at Ryerson Polytechnic Institute before moving to New York in 1985 to start his photography studio. Bill is a still life, food and portrait photographer, with many of his works appearing in several publications including *TIME*, *Musician Magazine*, *GUSTO!*, *Computer Life* and *Gourmet*. In 1995, *Better Homes and Gardens* published a complete set of three books detailing the spirit of Christmas with over 200 of Bill's photographs of specialty crafts and beautiful food presentations. Bill's assignments frequently take him to locations throughout the U.S., in addition to many trips to Toronto and Europe. In 1996 Bill accepted over 125 location assignments outside of New York. He can be reached at www.billmilne.com

♀ mercer digital design

When we were first shown Generation Eats, we got excited. All we really saw was a list of recipes but we could tell by their names that we wanted to eat them — and so we wanted to design the book. It wasn't hard to design — just make those oh so cool recipe names as big as possible and let everything else flow together. The end result is a pretty funky little cookbook and huge hunger pains! P.S. If you want to contact us our phone number is (416) 596-9199 or drop us a line at 388 King Street, West, Suite 111, Toronto, Ontario M5V 1K2. You can even Email us at 76001.1413@compuserve.com. Include a favorite photo of your pooch — we love dogs!

Global Film Services

Global Film Services was very pleased to help in the digital photography, imaging and proofing stages of this project. With the great art direction and photography talent, we feel that Generation Eats has a flavor that will appeal to everyone. Global Film resides at www.globalfilm.com

Amy Rosen is a Toronto-based freelance journalist who is in her twenties and is embarrassed by her choice of the book's title, although it does make its point. She has a B.A. in Film and Communications from McGill University, a Bachelor of Journalism degree from the University of King's College, and a Certificate in Basic Cuisine from Le Cordon Bleu Paris Cooking School. She writes about food, health, film, and new media for publications such as *TV Guide*, *Maclean's* magazine, *Shift* magazine, and *Chatelaine* magazine. She's always looking for new gigs and projects, so drop her a line if you're hiring. This is her first book, and she hopes you thoroughly enjoy it.